POLITICS O

Andrew Samuels is Professor of Analytical Psychology at the University of Essex and Visiting Professor of Psychoanalytic Studies at Goldsmiths College, University of London. He is a Training Analyst of the Society of Analytical Psychology and a Scientific Associate of the American Academy of Psychoanalysis. In addition to his London-based private practice in psychotherapy, he also works internationally as a political consultant. He is joint founder of Psychotherapists and Counsellors for Social Responsibility and of Antidote, the psychotherapy-based think tank. His previous books have been translated into eighteen languages. They include *Jung and the Post-Jungians*; *A Critical Dictionary of Jungian Analysis* (with Bani Shorter and Fred Plaut); *The Father*; *The Plural Psyche*; *Psychopathology* and *The Political Psyche*.

Also by Andrew Samuels

Jung and the Post-Jungians
The Plural Psyche: Personality, Morality and the Father
The Political Psyche
A Critical Dictionary of Jungian Analysis
(with Bani Shorter and Fred Plaut)
The Father (ed.)
Psychopathology (ed.)

POLITICS ON THE COUCH

Citizenship and the Internal Life

ANDREW SAMUELS

P

PROFILE BOOKS

First published in Great Britain in 2001 by
Profile Books Ltd
58A Hatton Garden
London ECIN 8LX
www.profilebooks.co.uk

Copyright © Andrew Samuels, 2001

Typeset in Minion by MacGuru
info@macguru.org.uk

Printed and bound in Great Britain by
Biddles Ltd
www.biddles.co.uk

The moral right of the author has been asserted.

Cover image: de Chirico, Giorgio, *The Enigma of a Day* (1914).
Oil on canvas, 73¼ x 55 in (185.5 x 139.7 cm).
The Museum of Modern Art, New York. James Thrall Soby Bequest.
Photograph © 2001 The Museum of Modern Art, New York.

A CIP catalogue record for this book is available from the British Library.

ISBN 1 86197 219 9

For my clients

Everything starts in mysticism and ends in politics.
Charles Péguy

Contents

Preface

I N A sense, *Politics on the Couch* is the final volume of a trilogy that began with *The Plural Psyche* (1989) and continued with *The Political Psyche* (1993). Though this book is an extension of the attempts made in the previous two to map the links between our inner and outer worlds, between the seemingly opposite realms of psychotherapy and politics, it is also at times an argument with its predecessors. Much in it has been stimulated by reactions to the ideas I offered previously.

Politics on the Couch is the most ambitious of the three volumes in that it represents my attempt to work out a new language in which the goals of the other two could have been expressed had I had the words at my disposal.

Like all writers, I have been wondering about how the book will be read. Will it be read as a text written by a professor or by a psychotherapist? These two roles have very different approaches to truth and the relative weight given by each to the emotions and their bearing on personal conduct is also different. For the therapist, the acid test is how an individual experiences things 'inside', how he or she dreams, relates and behaves in the personal realm. For the academic, while these may be important matters, the overall emphasis is – well, academic.

Will the book be seen as written by a person who is primarily a therapist or by a citizen who just happens to be a therapist? Sometimes people say to me, 'Well, that's very interesting and useful but you don't really need to be a therapist to say something like that. Shouldn't you have a special therapy perspective on these matters?' Others say, 'Well, I'm sure professional therapists and analysts will be interested in your ideas, but what practical political use will they have?' I have become practised at dealing with such responses, for example, on several occasions when organizing and speaking at fringe meetings at Labour Party conferences in the 1990s. Sometimes, I have heard both responses to the same talk.

Part of the problem is that psychotherapy and its ways of thinking are not greatly respected, or welcomed into public conversations. Therapists are often seen as lacking a sense of the real world and therefore as having no credibility. Yet the politicians and commentators who hold sway have not done such a great job of defining or running our political culture that they can afford to reject new approaches out-of-hand.

And will this book be read as a 'Jungian' text? In *The Political Psyche*, having attempted to assess Jung's anti-Semitism, I made the suggestion that contemporary Jungian analysts make reparation for what Jung said and did. The suggestion has been taken up by many colleagues and, together, we have looked at the whole spectrum of Jung's theories to see if they need modifying or throwing away. Having subjected Jung's ideas about culture and the psyche to a critical analysis, I now feel free to incorporate those that I *do* feel are relevant and useful.

As far as my professional identity is concerned, however, I would prefer to be thought of as a psychotherapist with a post-Jungian training and background. In psychoanalytic circles, and in the intellectual world generally, to be tagged 'Jungian' still carries a certain taint and leads people to regard one's work as suspect. So let me say it plainly: this is not a 'Jungian' book and should not be read as such. It should be judged on its own merits. Or, to paraphrase a sentence often found in prefaces, any errors in this book are mine and not C. G. Jung's.

Finally, the experiential basis for this book lies in my involvement with a number of political organizations and recent political developments. I have carried out consultations and conducted workshops with politicians, political organizations, activist groups and members of the public in Britain, the United States, Brazil, Israel and South Africa designed to explore how useful and effective perspectives derived from psychotherapy might be in the formation of policy, in new ways of thinking about the political process and in the resolution of conflict. It is difficult to present therapeutic thinking about politics so that mainstream politicians – for example, a Democratic senator or a Labour Party committee – will take it seriously. And the problem is not much reduced when the politicians and organizations are 'alternative'. But it can be done. From time to time, in *Politics on the Couch*, what I have experienced, witnessed and discovered in these workshops and consultations provides an experiential foundation for my arguments.

I have also been involved in the formation of three organizations engaged in some of the activities discussed in this book. Psychotherapists and Counsellors for Social Responsibility is an organization intended to help therapists and counsellors use their knowledge and experience to intervene as professionals in social and political matters. The second organization is Antidote, a psychotherapy-based think-tank.

It fosters multidisciplinary work, and links are sought with people working in fields other than psychotherapy. Antidote has undertaken research work into psychological attitudes to money and economic issues and is also involved in trying to apply ideas about emotional literacy to politics.

The third organization was the St James's Alliance (which no longer exists). Based at a church in central London, it consisted of individuals from diverse fields such as politics, economics, ethics, religion, non-governmental organizations, the media and psychotherapy. It attempted to incorporate ethical, spiritual and psychological concerns into the British political agenda and facilitate a dialogue between non-governmental organizations, single issue groups and activist organizations. It was an experiment in gathering and using political energy that is normally split up and dissipated.

I hope it is apparent that I believe that many ideas and practices of psychotherapy will need to change if therapists want to be taken seriously by politicians. I suggest some of the ways in which psychotherapists need to reform in order to make a useful contribution to public life, or expect anyone to listen when they try.

The book opens with two chapters that set out a stall, arguing for the value of an approach to politics deriving from psychotherapy and explaining the main principles of transformative politics. Chapters 3, 4 and 5 use gender, sexuality and the 'internal family' to chart and advocate new attitudes to the political process and inquire into the origins of political change. Chapters 6 and 7 discuss 'good-enoughness' in politics, with reference, first, to leadership and next to fatherhood. Then there are five chapters on political themes: the politics of spirituality, economics, how to use the values and practices of psychotherapy for political ends, relations between citizens and the state, and national psychologies. Finally, Chapter 13 highlights and extends the main themes of the whole book.

Acknowledgements

I am once again grateful for a generous grant from the Ann and Erlo van Waveren Foundation in New York.

I am extremely grateful for the help from many people I have received while writing this book, including Mike Adams, John Beebe, Clarissa Pinkola Estes, Jo Foster (for her usual impeccable word processing), Andrew Franklin (Profile Books), Tom Kirsch, Susie Orbach, Renos Papadopoulos, Rosie Parker, Fred Plaut, Sonu Shamdasani, Tom Singer, John Southgate, Martin Stanton, David Tresan and Luigi Zoja. Special thanks go to Evelyn Toynton for her meticulous and challenging editing.

Responsibility for the views expressed is, of course, mine.

All of the chapters were written with the book in mind. However, some chapters or sections were published as work-in-progress, as follows: 'Retraining the psyche: psychological reflections on the new labour economics', *Journal of the British Institute for Integrative Psychotherapy*, Vol. 2, 1994; 'A new therapy for politics/a new politics for therapy', *Self and Society*, Vol. 2, No. 6, 1995; 'The good-enough father of whatever sex', *Feminism and Psychology*, Vol. 5, No. 4, 1995; 'In praise of gender confusion', *Soundings: A Journal of Politics and Culture*, Vol. 2, 1996; 'Politics and psyche: can psychotherapists make a difference?', *Forum of the New Zealand Association of Psychotherapists*, Vol. 3, 1997; '"And if not now, when?": spirituality, psychotherapy, politics', *Journal of Psychodynamic Counselling*, Vol. 4, No. 3, 1998.

Acknowledgement is due to A.P. Watt Ltd. on behalf of Michael B. Yeats for permission to include the poem 'The Great Day' by W.B. Yeats.

Politics on the Couch

CHAPTER ONE

The secret life of politics

POLITICS IN many Western countries is broken and in a mess: we urgently need new ideas and approaches. This book argues that psychotherapy can contribute to a general transformation of politics. Therapists can ignore the demoralization in the political realm and continue to focus on personal transformation. Or they can try to transform self-concern into social and political concern, thereby helping to revitalize politics.

Today's politicians leave most of us with a sense of deep despair and disgust. They lack integrity, imagination and new ideas. Across the globe, a search is on to remodel politics. Psychotherapy's contribution to this search depends on opening up a two-way street between inner realities and the world of politics. We need to balance our attempts to understand the secret politics of the inner world of emotional, personal and family experiences with attempts to reveal the secret psychology of pressing outer world matters such as leadership, the economy, environmentalism and nationalism.

These are the sorts of questions that need answering:

❖ How happy are we with the current visions of political

'reality' on offer and the way the major political parties seem to see the future?

❖ Do we agree with the goals that politicians set?

❖ Can we do better? If so, what must change in us as individuals, as well as in society?

❖ How must our political system alter to regain the respect of alienated, excluded groups and individuals, including young people generally?

If people sharpen their half-thought-out, intuitive political ideas and commitments, then they are more able to take effective political action when they want to. Their desire to do so will also increase. There are buried sources of political wisdom within everyone. These are found in the private reactions we have to what is going on in the political world. Yet such private reactions have no obvious outlet and therefore tend to remain secret. This book will explore the ways in which secret things, the kind that are usually regarded as supremely private, such as childhood experiences, intimate relationships, fantasies (including sexual fantasies), dreams and bodily sensations, might be reframed and turned to useful and transformative political ends.

Our inner worlds and our private lives reel from the impact of policy decisions and the existing political culture. Why, then, do our policy committees and commissions not have a psychotherapist sitting on them as part of a spectrum of experts? This is not a call for a committee of therapists! But just as a committee will often have a statistician present, whose role might not always be fully appreciated by the other members, so, too, there should be a therapist at the conference table. You would expect to find therapists having views to offer on social issues that involve personal relationships.

The media regularly feature discussions about whether and how men can be nurturing figures and the extent to which political alliances between women and men are possible. But there are also some hard areas of political life (the economy, leadership, nationalism) that, surprisingly and increasingly, are being looked at from a psychotherapy point of view. These are reviewed in the course of the book.

Phrases like 'emotional intelligence' and 'emotional literacy' encapsulate calls for an increase in self-knowledge. But such phrases can be taken as addressing more than the private side of life. Modern society plunges us into a condition of uncertainty in which we often lose track of what we feel and slip into states of depression and helplessness. The idea of emotional literacy can be extended into the public sphere, so that we can envision a citizenry wanting to engage with politics in a feeling-based way, secure in the knowledge that they will still be coherent.

One poignant contribution that a psychotherapy viewpoint might make to political life is to help people face up to the inevitability of disappointment. It is one of the more valuable outcomes of psychotherapy, derived from the struggles experienced in the process itself: people realize that it is possible to gather the strength to push through the despair barrier and struggle on.

Many individuals involved in psychological work hold that politics is a disgusting business, and that getting involved in it sullies one, inevitably leading to a loss of self-respect. Professional psychotherapists often have little time for politics. Equally, many politicians, mainstream or activist, scorn introspection and psychological reflection as a waste of time. We need to question the conventional wisdom that there is a divide between the political life and what we usually understand as personal creativity. Might it be possible to be effective in politics without losing self-respect? Certainly the stakes are high: by not responding to the crisis in politics, we risk losing a place in political life altogether. Such matters will then be left to the media – whose own use of psychology seems more like a symptom than a potential cure.

The media's star columnists and pundits certainly toss around psychological terms when discussing politicians' behaviour. But mostly they are just engaging in pseudo-psychological analyses of the 'character' of our leaders, attempting to explain how they got that way: was it Bill Clinton's alcoholic stepfather who made him over-anxious to please everybody? Did Winston Churchill's sense of being unloved by his beautiful mother and awareness of his father's failures give him the hunger to win public acclaim? It is a fruitless exercise, a parallel spectacle to that of the politicians themselves when they offer up their simplistic nostrums about 'virtue' and 'vision'. Just as we can no longer look to leaders for what is required, we cannot rely on the media to give us insight into the political process. Instead, we are thrown back on ourselves.

However fascinating it may be to play the parlour game of speculating on the psychological motivations of today's politicians, it may be more significant to find out what would happen to the political system if citizens were to work on their own political self-awareness – if they found what is called in this book 'the politician within'. Then there would be a different basis from which to question the motivations of politicians.

Politics will always be about power and the struggle for power, about the contest for control of resources, the conflict of sectional interests. But politics nowadays encompasses a crucial interplay between the public and private dimensions of power. This insight, which used to be the possession of an intellectual and academic elite, is poised to enter mass consciousness; these days, the political *has* become personal. Politics of both a destructive and a creative kind show up in family patterns, gender relations, connections between wealth and (mental) health, control of information and accompanying imagery, and in religious and artistic assumptions. More and more people are becoming aware of this.

Equally, politics itself has always been psychological, but the fact that it is a psychological or emotional business is usually presented as an unhappy state of affairs, something to be overcome or disowned. 'Irrational' responses to demagogues like Hitler are cited, as though most political responses were, or should be, purely rational. Attitudes would be different if we learned to trust and to understand our psychological responses to political events.

Whether one looks at the microcosm of an individual in a local community or the macrocosm of the global village, we are flooded with psychological themes, often of an apocalyptic nature. Thinking about fundamentalism, nationalism, ethnic cleansing, poverty, planetary despoliation, child abuse and the war of the sexes might make one want to give up on the human psyche. But – and this is where the idea of therapy comes in – we could begin to work out why we can be so destructive and unpleasant. As in therapy, we can pause in our rush to judge our political performance and reflect on its psychological roots. Politics embodies the psyche of a people. If there are creative and benevolent aspects to that psyche that do not show up in the political life of a people, then we must ask 'why?'

At the beginning of the enterprise called psychotherapy,

the founders felt themselves to be social critics as much as personal therapists. As early as 1913, Freud said that psycho-analysis had the capacity

> to throw light on the origins of our cultural institutions, on religion, morality, justice and philosophy. Our knowl-edge of the neurotic illness of individuals has been of much assistance in our understanding of the great social institutions.[1]

In 1946, in a collection of essays on Nazi Germany, Jung wrote that

> We are living in times of great disruption. Political pas-sions are aflame, internal upheavals have brought nations to the brink of chaos. This critical state of things has such a tremendous influence on the psychic life of the individ-ual that the analyst feels the violence of its impact even in the quiet of his consulting room. The psychologist cannot avoid coming to grips with contemporary history, even if his very soul shrinks from the political uproar, the lying propaganda and the jarring speeches of the demagogues. We need not mention the analyst's duties as a citizen which confront him with a similar task.[2]

The great founders of humanistic psychology, such as Abraham Maslow, Carl Rogers and Fritz Perls, recognized the same thing – that they had in their hands a tool of social criticism and a possible agent of social change for the better, just as much as something that would help individuals in emotional difficulties.

In the 1920s and beyond, the Frankfurt School tried to marry Freud and Marx.[3] Wilhelm Reich also situated his work in the space between communism and psychoanalysis and R. D. Laing was in a similar tradition. Increasingly, in the 1990s, psychoanalysts began again to think about society, as the titles of their books show: *The Analyst in the Inner City*, or *Constructing the Self, Constructing America*.[4] Then there are feminist psychotherapists (such as Susie Orbach) and gay affirmative counsellors (like Claudette Kulkarni) whose work necessarily incorporates a social perspective.[5] Many therapists work in social and communal institutions and have brought psychodynamic insights to clinical engagements with people living in poverty. Not all therapy work has been done with the well heeled.

So the project of linking therapy and the world is clearly not a new one. Yet very little progress seems to have been made. To play with the title of a much-cited critique of psychotherapy, we have had a hundred years of psychotherapy's desire to change the world, but the world has stayed pretty much the same.[6]

More therapists than ever want psychotherapy to realize the social and political potential that its founders perceived in it. But there is a large gap between wish and actuality, between wanting to play a role in social and political life and actually playing that role and getting results. We need to acknowledge that anybody, not just a therapist, who seeks to improve anything is up against massive impersonal forces that do not want change: the economic system, the workings and institutions of global capitalism, patriarchy and its ways. But there is another, more paradoxical problem: the human unconscious and the human soul are the sources of imagination, creativity and hope, but they are also the sources of our problems. In its cruel and negative aspects, the unconscious resists improvement and change and contributes to the

difficulties human beings face. This could be seen as a therapist's philosophy of life. The very thing that gives us hope
that solutions might be found is also the source of the problems that cry out for solutions.

There are also other reasons, entrenched in the history of
psychotherapy and its institutions and practices, that have
blighted the hopes that therapists have long nurtured to
provide therapy for the world. In asking ourselves why the
world did not turn up for its first session, we need to acknowledge the role of the seemingly incurable psychotherapeutic reductionism and triumphalism that parallels that of
the media. Psychotherapists write articles for newspapers
about the phallic symbolism of cruise missiles going down
ventilator shafts in Baghdad or they call Mrs Thatcher a
restorative container for British infantile greed. Jungians go
in for an archetypal version of reductionism – the military-
industrial complex as the work of the Greek god Hephaestus,
feminism as the legacy of Artemis. What is the point of this?
Maybe the world was right not to turn up. It is startling,
when talking politics with therapists, how strong the desire is
to have psychotherapeutic theories proved right – stronger,
sometimes, than the initial desire to make a contribution.

One reason for therapists' failure to make a difference is
their tendency to split off their social analysis and social criticism from their clinical knowledge. There has been a big
divide between the therapist as social critic and the therapist
as clinical professional working with an individual, family,
couple or group. This is a terrible mistake: if therapists do
not bring in their clinical experience, their special knowledge, then why should anybody listen to what they say? Clinical work constitutes what marketing people call the USP –
unique selling point – when it comes to social criticism. It is

more than a question of therapists using what they hear from clients in an evidential way. It is also about seeing how the inner world of emotion and fantasy builds up in a ceaseless feedback loop with the outer world. It involves understanding that outer world problems contain emotional and fantasy elements as well, and seeing how the political and the psychological mutually irradiate. As we shall see, the practices and techniques of clinical psychotherapy can be claimed for a new model of transformative politics.

A second reason for failure has to do with psychotherapy's very bad record over the years at 'governing the soul', to use the caustic phrase of sociologist Nikolas Rose.[7] One does not have to give up therapy work (like James Hillman), or write a book against therapy (like one-time psychoanalyst Jeffrey Masson), or launch attacks on 'therapism' (like novelist Fay Weldon), to note that many attempts by therapists to work in the social domain have been disasters. Consider the bungled attempts by therapists to deal with shell shock and battle neurosis in the First World War (memorably depicted in Pat Barker's novel *Regeneration*), or the cultural biases of psychological testing, or various therapists' co-operation with oppressive regimes – including Jung's ambivalent relationship with anti-Semitism and Nazi ideology.

Then there is the whole question of therapy's weddedness to normative and universalistic standards in relation to gender, parenting and sexuality. The psychotherapy profession still fails – appallingly – to thoroughly depathologize homosexuality, for instance, or to offer realistic support to lone-parent families. With all the talk around the world of multiculturalism and biculturalism, the claim of psychotherapy to universality is damaging. Yet it is difficult to get beyond it, to come to terms with the idea that the Oedipus complex may be characteristic only of fin-de-siècle Vienna, and Jung's belief that women should not wear trousers pure 'Zürichocentrism'.

In spite of this depressing litany, there are some grounds for cautious optimism. The definition of politics is changing to make more of a place for psychology. Similarly, how we define spirituality and the aspirational side of life is also being revised in a more social or political direction. Even the breakdown of language in this sphere may in fact present us with an opportunity of sorts. I refer to the way that the language of the heart (inner world language) and the language of politics (outer world language) have become so separate that to mingle them sounds like embarrassing woolly-headedness. We have a chance to create a new, hybrid language and to practise using it.

A further ground for cautious optimism is that the politics of difference with which many Western societies are presently engaged have started to spawn a psychology of difference based on experience, rather than on definition. That means trying to understand the actual experience of being a Jew or Irish or a Maori or a woman or a lesbian or a man or a gay man or a child – not an attempt to define what these people *are* but an exploration of what being one of them is *like*. A psychology can be fashioned from the experiences, testimonies and stories of these groups (which are not, of course, homogeneous monoliths themselves).

In addition, the psychotherapy profession is beginning to pay more attention to its own political problems and biases, such as the historic discrimination against homosexuals, or the professional hierarchies which have ossified over the years. Issues such as improving access to treatment and training for members of minority groups, those without conventional academic qualifications, and people without many financial resources, are firmly on the agenda these days – although there has been a lot of opposition to it.

As far as psychotherapy reductionism is concerned, a shift is taking place in favour of multidisciplinary work. There are attempts in many disciplines to find linkages with psychotherapy and its underlying psychologies; for example, in religious studies, sociology, art history and theory, and even fields such as law and theoretical physics. These disciplines are linking up, not only with psychotherapy but also with each other, in ways that the conventional Western academy could not have imagined even in the mid-1970s.

Moreover, the nature of knowledge is changing, and this is a key theme for the twenty-first century: tacit, intuitive, feeling-based or fantasy-derived heuristic knowledge is finding a new welcome even in bastions of rationalist Enlightenment thought such as universities. The role of experience in learning is increasingly being valued as teachers and lecturers realize that a lowering of standards is not necessarily involved.

Finally, psychotherapy's ability to contribute to political life may be helped if it gains acceptance as a viable mode of treatment. The persistent suspicion that psychotherapy simply does not work has been one of the reasons for its manifest unpopularity. In recent years there have been numerous research findings that suggest that it can alleviate people's psychological distress. As information about this research percolates, greater general acceptance of psychotherapy should result.[8]

But whatever the grounds for optimism, there is still a huge problem with mapping therapy on to society: no consensus exists about the relationship between psychological and social phenomena. Those with a materialist outlook would assert that the psychological realm is utterly subordinate to the nitty-gritty economic forces that have inexorably constructed our world. Conversely, there are psychotherapists and psychoanalysts (and possibly poets) who believe that the psyche (or unconscious) is the dominant force, decisively colouring and shaping the apparently external social world. According to this view of things, psychology is primary, while the social world is actually an ensouled one – *anima mundi*, soul in and of the world. Social and material aspects of our world, and the suffering to which they lead, are therefore only secondary phenomena. The materialists insist that exactly the opposite is true.

Meanwhile, holistic thinkers, particularly during the 1980s and 1990s, have argued that the boundaries between the social and psychological realms are illusory – just as boundaries between the inner and outer worlds are illusory. In the same way, the ecopsychologists dispute, sometimes over-facilely, the idea that there is any boundary between human and non-human sources of emotional distress.[9]

A more dialectical approach would be to see the psychological and the social in fluid, ceaseless, unending, unresolvable interplay. Or a pluralist might argue that the relations between the psychological and the social consist of all of the above. It just depends on the context, on who is talking, and on what he or she wants to do with those ideas.

It is possible that the relations between the psychological/personal and the social/collective levels of reality cannot be fully grasped via any of the approaches just outlined. There may be a missing element in both our psychological and our political thinking and language. This is the most challenging and difficult possibility. One of the chief aims of this book is to try to help fumble a way towards an understanding of what that missing element might consist of. Future generations will be much better than we are at providing what is missing and speaking the new hybrid language of politics and therapy that is being born.

The birth of such a language is demonstrated in this brief clinical vignette. Riccardo, an Italian businessman of 35, had a dream in which there was a powerful image of a beautiful mountain lake with deep, clear, crystalline water. The client's first association was that the lake was a symbol of his soul, or at least the potential in him to develop a deep, clear attitude to life. His next association was to the pollution on the Adriatic coast of Italy which had clogged up the coastal waters with algae and weeds. He began to explore the possible connections between 'soul' and 'pollution'. Can one's soul remain deep and clear while there is pollution in one's home waters? How could the lake, mysterious and isolated, relate to mass tourism being damaged by algae in the Adriatic?

Then the client posed the question: who owns the lake? Who should control access to such a scarce resource? Who was responsible for protecting the lake's beauty from pollution? From personal issues, such as how his problems interfered with the development of his potential, he moved to political issues such as pollution, environmental despoliation and the degradations of mass tourism. And he then moved back again from the political level to the personal one. The dream played a part in Riccardo's choice to return to Italy, tell his parents that he was gay and, in his words, get 'involved' in some kind of politics.

Working these forbidden zones shows that it is legitimate and necessary to question the conventional boundaries between the public and the private, the political and the personal, the external world and the internal world, being and doing, extraversion and introversion, and between politics and psychology – between the fantasies of the political world and the politics of the fantasy world.

CHAPTER TWO

The politics of transformation

SINCE 1990, interest in exploring the boundary between psychotherapy and politics has grown enormously. Self-expression and self-development – the inward-looking perspectives of psychotherapy – and political activity can be seen as fulfilling similar functions. Self-expression may lead to political engagement, and political engagement may be part of a citizen's self-expression. A person may dream about starvation in Africa and decide to get involved in famine relief. Or a personal protest against childhood injustices will seek a concrete political format.

Politicians have always won elections by intuiting that, for millions of people, political choices, as expressed by voting, are matters of self-exploration and self-expression. When people who are not professional politicians look at their lives in terms of political ideas and commitments, they see an unfolding of their personalities in political terms. The politician within walks in a space that is neither wholly external and public, nor wholly internal and private, and is driven by a particular kind of political energy.

POLITICAL ENERGY

Jung noted that psychic energy was not confined in its expression to sexuality alone. He considered that energy flowed down 'channels', citing biological, psychological, spiritual and moral channels. If there were also to be a political channel for energy, what would it involve? Political energy involves bringing imaginative creativity to bear on seemingly intractable problems, trying to solve them in ways that reflect a concern for social justice, however that might be defined. Hence there are usually moral and spiritual aspects to it as well. Imagine a computer graphic designed to show the location and quality of political energy in a modern country. The screen glows red in those places where political energy is to be found and pulsates in step with its intensity. Where would we see bright, flashing red lights? In the formal political institutions, in local and national capitals, in the military, in banks and factories? Probably not. True, all of these are the traditional repositories of political *power* and, true, they still control the economic and other resources – such as information – that make a complex modern society tick. But the real political energy has left such places and gone elsewhere. Politics has left its home base and gone out into the world to redefine itself and find other and new places to settle. Political energy is not the same as political power.

I am not advocating removing political energy from its moribund institutions. It is happening anyway. All one can do is to chronicle and struggle to comprehend what may be the most significant sociocultural shift to take place in the Western countries since the end of the Second World War. A striking feature of the 1980s and 1990s in modern societies was the spontaneous growth of new social and cultural networks. More and more people are now involved in such networks – increasingly aware that what they are doing may be regarded as political. For example, we have seen movements that call for more enlightened environmental policies, more equitable arrangements for world trade, rights for ethnic and sexual minorities, animal liberation, dedication to organic farming, increased availability of complementary medicine including therapy and counselling. Others have become part of spiritual and religious movements that contain an implicit critique of existing society, or engaged in rock and other kinds of counter-cultural music and art, or pursued alternative and generally anti-capitalist lifestyles. The membership of such groups and movements runs into the millions, far more than are actively involved with the great political parties. In fact, every now and then a political party (the Democrats in the United States, the Liberals in Britain) will try to harness the rainbow energy in these developments and turn it into votes. But something usually goes wrong when the parties try to assimilate the new social movements.

The elasticity in our changing image of politics has not been brought about by intellectual theorists, but is something the very idea of politics seems actively to embrace. These social movements operate in isolation from each other, with seemingly quite different agendas and programmes. Because they do not operate within an alliance or coalition, they can show up on our computer graphic only as little scarlet pimpernels scattered across the country. Yet their collective illumination, if we could garner it, measure it – and do so without interfering with their activities – may be what Western societies, starved of creativity and imagination in their politics, crave and need as we stumble into the new century.

Furthermore, these disparate social movements have something *psychological* in common. They all emotionally reject big politics, its pomposity and self-interest, its mendacity and complacency. They share a philosophy or set of values based on ideas of living an intelligible and purposeful life in spite of the massive social forces that mitigate against intelligibility and purpose. They are all committed to a transformation of politics, which can be called the 'resacralization' of politics – that is, making politics holy, which involves attempting to get a sense of purpose, decency, aspiration and meaning back into political culture. (Even if such a state of political affairs never really existed, we behave and think as though it did – hence *re*sacralization.) Political reformers and resacralizers share a disgust with our present politics and politicians – sometimes it is literal disgust, the gagging reflex, an ancient part of the nervous system, absolutely necessary for survival in a world full of toxins. At workshops that explore psychological aspects of politics, participants often express disgust with politics with the accompanying symptom of retching.

A transformation of politics at the start of a new millennium is not going to happen in a simple and speedy way. It may not happen at all, given the uncontrollability of the social realm of existence. Furthermore, many would dispute that the cumulative public significance of these developments is positive. Is not the proliferation of new networks and cultural practices merely a symptom of social malaise – a selfish retreat into personal, individual preoccupations, reflecting an abandonment of the aspiration to truly political values? Finally – and it is a good argument – reactionary fundamentalist religious movements can also be seen as resacralizing. But what gets highlighted when religious funda-

18

mentalism is brought into the picture is the vastness of the energy pool available for the political reforms that are urgently needed. The director of a university centre for the study of cultural values and environmental change once asked bluntly how ideas like mine differed from something like pop singer Michael Jackson's 'Heal the World' concert. My reply was to suggest that, without the same pool of energy, his own centre would not have come into existence and achieved its remarkable success.

Progressive political people have managed to learn rather little from the political successes of the religious right and other conservative movements across the globe. While it would not be desirable to share their moralistic and simplistic approaches to life, it would be worthwhile trying to understand the kinds of yearnings that such movements seem to satisfy. It would be tragic if the most psychologically minded politicians were to turn out to be conservative leaders. The rigidity of religious fundamentalism shows it to be as scared of the uninhibited human imagination as are mainstream political institutions.

Words like 'spirituality' are politically neutral. The harnessing of spiritual passion and energy for politics is not in itself bound to lead to conservative outcomes. In fact, history tells us how radicalizing a force religions have also been over time, whether in promoting the rise of capitalism and the bourgeoisie, or as a source for socialist ideas, or of such important principles as passive resistance and non-violence. With these ideas in mind, reflection on the great political issues of the day and on politics itself allows a recognition to emerge that there really is no divide between the spiritual and the social, between the private and the public, between the inner life and the world of politics.

Hence we can read resacralization positively – as a healthy complement to the rapid decline in public identification with orthodox political institutions. (A recent poll indicated that two-thirds of the American population have no faith in the Congress or Presidency!) In fact, the future vitality of formal politics may depend on its ability to absorb resacralization. The resacralizing movements carry the seeds of new political forms that, much more than official politics, resonate with modern, culturally diverse societies, forms that imply a transformation of politics, or at least of political activity. This is the kind of politics that feminism prepared us for but did not take far enough in a psychological direction – a politics that goes beyond the level of what individuals know (the personal) to the level of what is not yet known (the unconscious), where the radical imagination sleeps.

A POLITICAL PSYCHE?

If we are to engage with issues of empowerment and disempowerment in a more psychological way, we have got to renegotiate what we mean by politics. In the late modern or postmodern Western world, the increased intermingling of ethnic, socioeconomic and national identity has meant that politics and questions of psychological identities are linked as never before. Forced and voluntary migrations make this inevitable. The whole picture is made more dense by the rapid course of events in the realms of gender, sexuality and sexual orientation. Because questions of gender exist on the threshold between inner and outer worlds (part of personal identity, part of social reality), it is not surprising that gender issues are central to any discussion of the transformation of politics.

It is not easy to make a psychological analysis of politics because every element in our culture is undergoing fragmentation and Balkanization. Still, people have risen to the challenge. The sense of complexity seems capable of increasing as well as damaging the possibility of political and social empowerment. For, in the midst of our tragic anomie and baffling atomization, the dreadful conformism of 'international' architecture, telecommunications and cuisine, the sense of oppression and fear of a horrific future, in the midst of war itself, there is occurring an equally strange and equally complex attempt at the transformation of politics.

Therapists are aware of this from what their clients tell them. Along with the expected problems – relationship difficulties, early traumas, feelings of emptiness – we see ecological and other crises presented as sources of symptoms and causes of unhappiness in individuals. From a psychological point of view, the world is making people unwell; it follows that, for people to feel better, the world's situation needs to change. But perhaps this is too passive: perhaps for people to feel better, they have to recognize that the human psyche is a political psyche and hence consider doing something about the state the world is in. (Consider Dorothea Brooke, in *Middlemarch*: constrained by all the Victorian conventions regarding women, she longs above all to be *useful* in the world, to have some small part in righting the social wrongs she sees around her. This impulse has probably not disappeared entirely since then.)

To test out the extent of the link between personal growth and political commitment, 2,000 analysts and therapists of many schools worldwide were surveyed about which political issues their clients mentioned in therapy. I asked how frequently the clients raised such issues, as well as how the analysts and therapists reacted and what their own political views were. Aside from revealing that the therapy profession is far more politically sensitive than one would think and that politics is a welcome theme in quite a few clinical offices, their answers made it clear that clients are raising economic, environmental, and gender-political issues in their therapy sessions much more than they used to. This development in the therapy world seems to justify the wider claim that, in our age, we are witnessing the emergence of a new kind of politics.

But what kind of political player or citizen needs to emerge to make the vision of a transformation of politics into something more tangible? To answer this question, it is necessary to formulate new models or paradigms of the citizen.

THE POLITICIAN WITHIN

The politician within each of us needs to be approached with respect and affection for his or her diversity. I want to avoid creating another monolith, a 'we' that does not exist in politics today. Who is the 'we' that so often creeps into books and speeches on both politics and psychology? Sometimes, and uncontroversially, this 'we' refers to those reading or listening to the words in the here-and-now. But at other times the use of the 'w' word may reflect the tendency of a white, Western, middle-class, heterosexual male to see himself as representative of everyone. 'We' have to be careful not to inflate ourselves into a generality, but instead to make it clear who 'we' mean when using the word.

Nowhere is this carefulness more necessary than in discussing what can be called 'political self-awareness'. Because of the impossibility of anyone giving an objective account of how they got their political attitudes and commitments, we might as well speak about the 'political myth of the self'.

Most often, as noted earlier, the psychological thrust into politics has focused on the psychology of the politician(s), that is their personality and likely behaviour in stressful situations and crises. Or there have been studies of the citizens, the voters, designed to help politicians appeal to or manipulate them. There has not been very much self-reflexive psychological work done in relation to politics, and this is where the experience garnered in clinical therapy practice becomes useful. For the resacralizing movements to be effective, we have to start believing in the possibility of a citizen whose individuation – in Jung's term, the process of becoming himself or herself, distinct from but related to others – has a political aspect to it.

In my view, unless ideas like these are embraced, there will be less chance of any transformation of politics. It will just have been another fad, a low-key reprise of the 1960s. Resacralization is at risk, not only because of the reactionary and cynical moves of patriarchal capitalists, but also because of something lacking in the kind of personalities typically involved in resacralization. All too often, resacralizers are reluctant to sacrifice self-respect by getting their hands dirty, and are therefore characterized psychologically by an attempt to construct a shadow-free politics. Leave the dirty stuff to the politicians, meaning the real politicians, not deep and profound people like us! The 'shadow' is a term coined by Jung to refer to those aspects of ourselves that we would like to disown – but cannot, because to have a shadow is part of being human. Shadow-free politics are often achieved by locating the problem elsewhere – in men, in whites, in the free market and so on. Then the belief of so many people in an apocalyptic end, whether through the greenhouse effect, an AIDS pandemic or nuclear conflagrations, can be understood as an attempt to shift the blame on to other people and institutions.

Many of us are so full of self-punishing contempt for ourselves, so full of disgust for the culture in whose making we have participated, that we opt for a thin, purist, over-clean style of making politics. We are so anxious not to be contaminated by the shadow that on one level we do not really want to see our cherished ideals translated into pragmatic politics. We fear that being effective means sacrificing our purity. Even when resacralizers do get involved in politics, it is often a half-hearted or incomplete involvement, psychologically speaking, characterized by the fear of being corrupted by ugly reality, and so not a truly creative engagement with the world and its problems. Hence the traumas of so many of the Green parties and groups, torn between their idealism and more pragmatic notions of feasibility. Sometimes it seems that Galsworthy was right when he said, 'Idealism increases in direct proportion to one's distance from the problem.'

Certainly, bringing transformative politics into contact with official politics creates a problem familiar to anyone who has ever had a political ideal. The closer one gets to the 'real world', with all its pressures, diversions and temptations, the more risk there is of the ideal becoming sullied, of its losing its purity, shape and impetus. Anyone active in environmentalism or the women's movement will confirm this. One role for a psychological commentator is to explore whether this is an inevitable process or whether there might be something of a psychological kind that we can do to achieve a better blend of idealism and realism.

Those who want to resacralize politics are often searching for something, some kind of self-fulfilment or self-actualization, that the conventionally political is never going to wholly supply. Anyone who was active in the New Left or in student politics will know about these issues. There was total denial of the human needs that were also being met (or not met), and of the all-too-human power struggles that were going on, as activists sat around for hours discussing what to paint on the banners to be held up outside car plants. In fact, it was regarded as apolitical and highly suspect to ask about personal motivations – people got booted out for it. The New Left of the 1960s failed its own people by outlawing sub-jectivity, and this may be one psychological reason why pro-gressive politics in the West is so lacklustre just now. When feminism took the opposite tack, encouraging people to say at length what their personal reasons were for turning up at the meeting, a gulf of style and ethos arose between femi-nism and other progressive political movements in the com-munity that has still not healed.

If we could work out ways of increasing political self-awareness, based on therapy work, then the fear of getting dirty hands and co-operating with people one does not exactly love might be addressed. Returning to our imaginary computer graphic, we could see if those little red dots might coagulate and eventually colour the screen red.

The various politically transformative groups tend to be interested in single issues. Hence they do not communicate, let alone coagulate. Nor have they formed themselves into any kind of coalition. Attempts have been made to organize meetings for members of the various groups and I have found the process at these meetings one of the most hopeful signs of political transformation. Often, members of different groups have not realized the degree of psychological similarity in their projects, or understood what they have in common. This becomes clear when, for example, a 'women and poverty' person meets and talks with a 'Christian ecology' person, or people involved in human rights organizations come into contact with ecofeminists. The psychological task is, first, to bring about a conversation and then to try to bring out the similarities of aim, often in emotional terms or as images, between the various enterprises. Affinities and possibilities for alliances can be pointed out without pretending that all the groups have to love each other wholeheartedly; all that is necessary is to make a temporary and partial alliance. *Why should the capitalists and the patriarchs be so good at this kind of deal-making and the resacralizers so bad at it?* Maybe the various groups of capitalists and patriarchs have been so effective precisely because they have sensed what they have in common behind surface differences.

One difficulty is the profound reluctance in the West to connect the outer, public levels of life with the inner, private levels. We assume that it is always the outer, public levels where connections will be made. Yet people have always spoken about politics and politicians in psychological terms such as 'character'. (Consider the outpouring of books on Richard Nixon.) Similarly, a good deal of political debate boils down to disagreement about what constitutes human nature (what, if anything, lies beyond self-interest, to give an example).

If we can accept that a connection exists between outer and inner worlds, we will get more used to talking the mixed language of psychology and politics described in the previous chapter. And we will want to know not only what is being said, but also who is saying it – and then exactly who is taking action. Therapists know that everyone teems with inner people ('sub-personalities') and that this is always a difficult thing for clients to acknowledge. In the same way, we need to develop an approach to politics that understands that no society provides a single, unified psychological identity for all its members.

An awareness that politics is psychological is one theme that links all of those engaged in the ongoing discussion about the loss of meaning, purpose and certainty in communal and personal life. Yet such is the fear of the inner world that its implications are barely recognized, let alone discussed or made use of. It is tragic how little discussion there has been about the socialized, transpersonal psychology that will be needed to make current visions of community (and communitarian) politics viable. But there *are* psychological theories in existence that focus on the transpersonal ways in which people are already linked and attuned to one another, living in connection in a social ether. In this vision of humanity, it is possible to recognize that we were never as separate from each other as so-called free market, neo-liberal political economy – which had its own tame psychological theory in there – claimed we were. Politicians and citizens urgently need to explore, expound and cultivate the kinds of pre-existing connections between people that Jung called the collective unconscious. Such connections may be largely non-verbal, working on a psyche-to-psyche level.

THE POLITICAL MYTH OF THE SELF

Individuals live not only their own individual lives but also the life of the times. (Jung is always quoted as telling his students that 'when you treat the individual you treat the culture'.) People cannot be seen in isolation from the society and culture that has played a part in forming them. What would happen, then, if we paid the same kind of attention we give to the inner life of the individual in therapy to what might be called his or her 'political selfhood'?

Once we see that there is a political self who has developed over time, we can start to track the political history of that self – the way the political events of a lifetime have contributed to forming the individual's political myth. It is possible to analyse the politics people have, so to speak, 'inherited' from their families and their class, ethnic, religious and national backgrounds – not forgetting the crucial questions of their sex and sexual orientation. Sometimes people take on their parents' politics; equally often, people reject what their parents stood for. There is a common experience of feeling oppressed by a domestic tyrant, whether male or female, or seeing other family members as oppressed that can give rise to a sharp sense of injustice and embryonic revolutionary feelings. Often, significant figures from outside the family – teachers, clergy, friends – are politically important. And key events – Vietnam, Suez and so forth – play an important role.

As far as socioeconomic background is concerned, it is clear that a relationship exists between class and the individual's inner world. Many people have achieved a higher socioeconomic status than their parents. And yet, in their inner worlds, encountered in therapy, the social class in which they function is often the social class into which they were born. A staggering psychological tension exists within socially and economically mobile citizens between what they are and what they were. To the extent that the typical move has been from working class to middle class, and to the extent that passion and the need for social and economic justice exist within the working class (for good reasons), it is possible to see the middle-class person's concern for economic and social justice as appropriate to their inner world version of themselves as working class.

Perhaps this account of how a person's political myth develops is a bit too rational. If there is something inherently political about humans, then maybe the politics a person has cannot be explained only by social inheritance. Maybe there is an accidental, constitutional, fateful and inexplicable element to think about. Maybe people are just born with different amounts and types of political energy inside them.

If that is true, it would have major implications both for individuals and for our approach to politics. What will happen if a person with a high level of political energy is born to parents with a low level of it (or vice versa)? What if the two parents have vastly different levels from each other? What is the fate of a person with a high level of political energy born into an age and a culture which does not value it, but prefers to reward lower levels of political energy? The answers to such questions shape not only the political person but also the tenor and flavour of the political scene.

The questions can get much more intimate. Did your parents foster or hinder the flowering of your political energy and your political potential? How did you develop the politics you have right now? In which direction are your politics moving, and why? There seems to be no political agenda, whether mainstream or alternative, that currently addresses these questions.

The point here is not about what might be called political maturity. No such universal exists, as is evidenced by the fact that different commentators evaluate the same groups as either 'terrorists' or 'freedom fighters'. What is essential is to discover how people got to where they are politically and, above all, how they themselves think, feel, explain and communicate about how they got to where they are politically – hence the political *myth* of the person. From a psychological angle, it often turns out that people are not actually where they thought they were politically, or that they got there by a route they did not know about. There is a political 'narrative truth' to consider as well as a political 'historical truth' (to use the terms of the American psychoanalyst Donald Spence).

As evidenced in radio phone-ins, newspaper correspondence columns and what is heard in therapy, people are becoming much more aware of and concerned by the gap between their private political histories, passions, dreams, ideas, feelings, bodily reactions to politics on the one hand and how policy is made and what happens in the political world on the other. This gap is disturbing and painful for all of us, but when things are disturbing and painful it also creates the opportunity for something creative to happen. Let us hope that citizens do not 'repress' their psychological need to be political because of these problems.

If a true dialogue between the two realms of inner reality and political reality cannot be managed, we could end up with an inward politics of self-righteous ineffectuality, full of rhetoric about soul and meaning but lacking any weight with the electorate or in the corridors of power. An overpsychological politics may ignore the outer world and not be politically realistic at all. We need psychological perspectives on pressing political problems in the real world – leadership, the market economy, Third World development, environmentalism, nationalism, racism and anti-Semitism. But we also need to lay bare the hidden politics of all those experiences and images in life that used to be comfortingly regarded as private.

One last dimension of the politician within concerns his or her 'political type'. The model here is Jung's typology: extroversion, introversion, thinking, feeling, sensation, intuition. For a variety of reasons, some of them to do with their personal backgrounds, some to do with their inborn political constitutions, people will live out the political aspects of themselves in different ways. Some will be violent terrorists; some pacifists. Some will want empirical back-up for their ideas; others will fly by the seat of their pants. Some will definitely enjoy co-operative activity; others will suffer the nightmare of trying to accomplish things in a group only because they passionately believe in the ends being pursued. As we begin to make a start on a psychologically driven transformation of politics, let us not make the mistake of insisting that everyone do it in precisely the same way. If we are to promote creativity, we need to value and honour diverse political types and styles, and to think of ways of protecting such diversity.

The notion of political types is particularly useful when addressing conflict, whether interpersonal or within organizations or between nations. Just as introverts and extroverts suffer from mutual incomprehension, people or groups of a particular political type often have very little idea how the other person or group is actually 'doing' politics. This is not to say that the political content *per se* is irrelevant, only that there may be more that divides opponents than their differing views. One might list different images of political types as follows: warrior, terrorist, exhibitionist, leader, activist, parent, follower, child, martyr, victim, trickster, healer, analyst, negotiator, bridge-builder, diplomat, philosopher, mystic, ostrich.

When considering one's political type or that of another, it is not necessary to stick to a single type. The context in which the politics in question are taking place needs to be borne in mind. Some people will be of one type in one setting and quite another in a different one. A negotiator at work may be a terrorist at home. Or people may have a 'superior' political type, an 'inferior' political type and an 'auxiliary' political type, to borrow Jung's terms. Thus a 'warrior' may have neglected his or her 'philosopher', which gets relegated to the inferior position. But the 'warrior' may have a 'parent' in an auxiliary role.

The list of types is organized along an active/passive spectrum and, when using political typology to orient oneself in respect of a particular conflict, it is noticeable that there is often a twinning between an overtly active and a covertly passive type within one of the disputants (or vice versa). For example, while conducting an experiential group composed of Israelis of Jewish and Arab background, it became clear that the very active – in this case, parental – attitude of some of the Jewish participants hid a really quite mystical approach to politics, one which almost welcomed a conflagration. Similarly, a dispute within a social welfare organization was illumined by the recognition that the victim-type politics of some staff members hid leadership and even warrior aspirations. In both situations, the warring elements were presented not with an analysis of *what* they were saying (that came later) but with a panorama of the *way* in which they were saying it, the type or style of politics they were utilizing. Family and marital conflicts, too, can be illumined by an understanding that disputants are speaking a completely different language, or at least dialect.

POLITICS AND 'HUMAN NATURE'

One specific political role for psychotherapists would be to mount a challenge to accepted ideas of what constitutes 'human nature'. At the moment, when idealistic or even utopian political thinking gets a bit threatening to the old order and to established ways of doing things, someone usually says: 'But what you're proposing goes against human nature!' What the speaker mostly means is that human nature is violent and greedy, involves hostility to other people and inevitably leads to a pecking order and social hierarchy. If such speakers are psychotherapists, it is usually assumed that they are experts in human nature and therefore particularly qualified to make this judgement.

But what if there is no such thing as an objective expert in human nature? Most statements on the subject reflect the social circumstances, ideological prejudices and individual personality of the writer – not to mention his or her purpose in writing. As Jung said, 'every psychology is a personal confession'. Moreover, the tag 'his or her' is very relevant because males and females are usually portrayed differently by writers on human nature – though what they say varies dramatically over time. For example, some ancient Greek philosophers said that women do not have souls. Apparently, up until the end of the eighteenth century it was considered perfectly manly for men in Europe to cry; then, according to novels and letters of the period, they were required to stop doing so.

In spite of these arguments, many people continue to assert the conservative proposition that human nature is the one thing that does not change over time. Yet the fact that people may always have had emotional and physical experiences does not mean that they experienced them in the same way. For the means they have to tell us about it are totally embedded in the worlds in which they lived. Hence it is very difficult to say that something is politically impossible on grounds of human nature. What therapists can contribute is an explanation of why the more positive aspects of human nature have such a struggle to emerge. They can also point out that the depressing definitions of human nature that abound are far from neutral. Someone always benefits from them: big business, conventional politicians, reactionary males, anyone with a stake in the system has an interest in preserving the system's conception of human nature, which implies that controls are necessary to prevent chaos and that reform is impossible. Ask who benefits when we are told that environmentalism and all kinds of new ideas for economic policy are unrealistic or too idealistic because of human nature's endemic greed and selfishness.

Some might dismiss this as New Age thinking. But none other than Oscar Wilde, who was not exactly New Age, said that 'The only thing we know about human nature is that it changes. Change is the one quality we can predict of it … The systems that fail are those that rely on the permanency of human nature, and not on its growth and development.'[1]

CHAPTER THREE

A new deal for women and men

T HE 'NEW DEAL' was the name given to the wide range of programmes, agencies and economic laws and institutions introduced by President Franklin Delano Roosevelt in the United States between 1933 and 1938. The term was also picked up by the Labour government in Britain in the 1990s. The new deal referred to in this chapter is a psychological as well as political new deal between the sexes. (It will be recalled that a person's sex is a key element in the formation of the politician within.) Roosevelt's economic and social reforms were responses to the trauma of the Great Depression. Who would disagree with the proposition that a traumatic situation has existed for women and men and the relations between them in most Western countries ever since the end of the Second World War?

'Gender' has come to mean the arrangements by which the supposedly biological raw material of sex and procreation is shaped by human and social intervention. Gender and the passionate politics it spawns have given rise to traumatic divisiveness in our world – West, East, South and North. But the very idea of gender also has a hidden bridge-building function: it sits on a threshold half-way between the inner and outer worlds, and thus is already half-way out into the world of politics. On the one hand, gender is a private, secret, sacred, mysterious story that we tell ourselves and are told by others about who we are. But it is also a set of experiences deeply implicated in and irradiated by the political and socioeconomic realities of the outer world. The notion of gender, therefore, not only marries the inner and outer worlds, but actually calls into dispute the validity of the division. It is no wonder, then, that gender issues get so politicized as well as continuing to turn us on, that contemporary political discussions focus so often on gender issues like the proportions of men and women in the various arms of government, paternity (as opposed to maternity) leave and the perennial issue of equality of pay.

MEN AND POLITICS

Ironically, men have become the object of much political and psychological scrutiny in the West these days and are often seen as 'the problem' – 'ironically' because for millennia men were the ones to scrutinize other groups and make them problematic: women, children, Blacks, the fauna and flora of the natural world. Men were a sort of papal balcony from which to survey the universe. But in our age, a huge shift in cultural consciousness has taken place and new questions about men have arisen: men as (errant) fathers, men as (violent) criminals, men as (uninvolved) citizens.

The three underlying questions seem to be: Can men change? Are men powerful? Do men hate women? Today's men and women would probably want to answer 'Yes and No' to all three of those questions. Saying 'Yes and No' is not a high-octane or passionate position, but it may be the only reasonable, viable, pragmatically effective and imaginative position to take.

Can men change? Men *can* change, of course, and yet the statistics about who typically takes care of children or does the washing-up show that they have not altered their behaviour very much. Why not? In the past few years, far too much time has been spent on irresolvable philosophical, metaphysical and quasi-scientific discussions about the relative importance of nature and nurture in the formation of gender identity and performance. Yet it may still be politically useful to consider the limitations on men's capacity to change – not because of putative biological hard-wiring but because of psychological factors, in psychotherapy language 'internalization', a kind of psychological rather than biological 'inheritance' referring to the way men take in (internalize) images of manliness they see projected by the outside world and make them part of their inner world.

Are men powerful? They certainly have economic power. But Black men, homeless men, men in prisons, young men forced or tricked into armies, disabled men, gay men – these are often vulnerable figures. We have serious trouble contemplating male economic power and male economic vulnerability simultaneously. We know, too, that men are scared of women. Never mind their fear of 'the feminine', what scares men is *women*. How can a man be said to be powerful if he is scared of women? And men are also frightened of other men. When contemplating the question of male power, what each of us has internalized is crucial in determining our answer – which means that personal experience and circumstances are decisive.

At the same time, the undoubted economic power that males possess could be made to serve progressive ends. If men and their formal institutions put just a tiny proportion of their economic power to benevolent use, it would make an enormous difference. So whatever changes may be taking place in the world of men could have immense political and social effects.

Do men hate women? Here, the word 'ambivalence' comes to mind and, as we shall return to the concept later, its history will be useful. In 1910, when Jung's superior, Eugene Bleuler, coined the word ambivalence, he meant it as a very serious symptom of schizophrenia. By the 1930s and 1940s, it had become *the sign* of psychological maturity according to psychoanalysis. Ambivalence is the capacity to have simultaneously hating and loving feelings towards the same person. So it is *not* only a problem, but an extremely hard-to-achieve aspect of psychological and social maturity. (Similarly, F. Scott Fitzgerald said that the test of a first-rate intelligence is the ability to hold two opposed ideas in the mind at the same time and still retain the ability to function.) Therefore, later in this chapter, when considering the creation of temporary deals and alliances of a political nature between men and women on the basis of their ambivalent feelings towards each other, something elevated, difficult to achieve and worthwhile is being proposed, not something tawdry and short term.

IN PRAISE OF GENDER CONFUSION

Most people are wary now of any individuals who seem too settled and sure in their gender identity and gender role. Think of the tycoon – so capable and dynamic, such a marvellous self-starter. Do we not know that, secretly, he is a sobbing little boy, dependent on others, perhaps mostly females, for all his feelings of safety and security? Or the Don Juan, talking incessantly of the women he has seduced, who turns out to have fantasies of being female himself and yearns to be seduced by another man? Or the woman who seems so fulfilled as a mother, yet privately desires to express herself in ways other than maternity, to come into another kind of power, to protest her cultural 'castration'?

We have come to accept that behind excessive gender certainty lurk gender confusions like these. At the same time, even many people who are suspicious of too much gender certainty feel that it is basically a good thing to be pretty certain about one's gender, to know for sure that, in spite of all the problems one has with being a man or a woman, one is indeed a man or a woman.

Yet it may be that another ideal altogether is needed to make sense of what we are experiencing in the muddled and mysterious world of early twenty-first-century gender relations and gender politics. Many people who come for therapy are manifestly confused about their gender identity. They may know how a man or woman is *supposed* to behave; but they are not sure that, given what they know about their internal lives, a person who is really a man or a woman could possibly feel or fantasize what they are feeling and fantasizing.

For these profound feelings of gender confusion to exist, there has to be an equally profound feeling of gender certainty in operation at some level – certainty based on the images presented by society. You cannot know the details of your confusion without having an inkling of the certitude against which you are measuring it. The client sobbing his little boy heart out knows very well that 'real' 'manly' tycoons exist out there and evaluates himself negatively as a result.

Indeed, we could even say: no gender certainty, no gender confusion. What this means is that, to a very great degree, people construct their gender confusion in relation to their gender certainty. If gender certainty is part of ordinary socialization, then gender confusion is equally constructed and not a deep personal wound or failure.

We need, therefore, to extend radically the by-now conventional insight that gender confusion lies behind gender certainty to see that *gender certainty lies behind gender confusion*. To the extent that gender confusion is usually taken as a mental health problem or neurosis, we are making a colossal mistake and even playing a destructive con trick on those supposedly suffering from it. The problem, in fact, is gender certainty.

We can look at how this operates for men in Western societies. The clichéd idea that many men living in a feminism-affected culture feel confused about who they are *as men* takes on a rather different cast if we disown the idea of the desirability of gender certainty. From this angle, modern men are not so confused – or at least feeling confused is not their main problem. Their problem is being afflicted with a gender certainty that is of no emotional use to them in their lives, and may be actually harmful to their potential. (When men's movement leaders offer a certainty that seems to have been missing from the lives of men, they are unwittingly doing nothing more than bringing the unconscious gender certainty that was always there to the surface and reinforcing it. As that certainty came from the culture in the first place, there is nothing radical or scene-shifting about it at all.)

The really interesting question is what to do with the feelings of gender confusion from which everyone suffers these days. It all becomes easier to live with if we replace the word 'confusion' with something that sounds more positive, like 'fluidity' or 'flexibility' or even 'androgyny'. But the word 'confusion' has merits because it comes closer to capturing what contemporary people feel about their gender identity.

In fact, gender confusion can contribute something valuable to political and social reform and change. If gender is a story we tell about ourselves that is half private and half public, it is also something upon which most polities have erected a welter of oppressive practices and regulations, mostly favouring men. Unfortunately, many Western governments (such as Labour in Britain) may be turning back to a retrogressive form of gender politics fuelled by the certitudinous 'family values' of the past, a politics which has always tended to favour men.

But many men want to make a progressive contribution to gender politics and hence (as men) to the wider political scene. It is not necessary to refuse to be a man, or enter into spurious sociopolitical alliances with women that deny the existence of differing political agendas for the sexes. All that may be required in the first instance is a celebration of not knowing too well who we are in terms of gender, not knowing too well what we are supposed to know very well indeed.

In workshops I have conducted on male psychology, participants engage in an exercise using a rating scale that represents a continuum from 'old man' to 'new man'. Old man counts as zero; new man counts as 10. If the person is a man, he is asked to place himself on this scale; if a woman, she is asked to score the most significant man in her life, past or present.

One might imagine that this would be a straightforward business, and people would respond by saying 6, 1, 2, 8 and so on. But it never happens like that. Many people insist on giving multiple answers. A man will say that he sees himself as a 2 *and* a 9. Sometimes this gets expressed more precisely: 'When I'm with a woman I'm more likely to be a 9, right at the new man end, but when I'm with men I find myself a 2 or a 3.'

One man said: 'I would say I'm a 2. I consider myself traditional, but I'm trying to modify myself.' The number of participants of both sexes who mention words like *modify, change, improve* in connection with men is very high. Another man said: 'When I thought about it, I thought 5. This isn't out of not wanting to change, but out of confusion – the struggle, uncertainty and confusion of being a man.'

Many women mock the exercise, but what they say is quite revealing. One woman said: 'I think my husband is a 2 but *he* thinks he's an 8.' Another woman said: 'I've been married for 33 years. My husband started as a 3 and after bringing up the children together, which was terribly important to him, I think he's become a … 4!'

We need to access what is involved in gender confusion and gender certainty in a new language of fleshly images that speak more directly to people's experience. Children seem to grasp this instinctively. When my son was 8 and my daughter 7, they taught me *their* theory of gender confusion, which has much more to do with self-image at depth than the more conventional, journalistic presentation of men as mixed up because of what women have managed to achieve. They identified four equal categories: boy-boy, boy-girl, girl-girl and girl-boy. Anatomy is important but not decisive in determining who belongs to which category. So my daughter could refer to herself as a girl-girl or a girl-boy while my son oscillated between being a boy-girl and a girl-boy. Context was important – it depended on whom they were with. This system gets beyond a simplistic heterosexual–homosexual or feminine–masculine divide. In the adult world, as many (or more) boy-girls are heterosexual as are homosexual. The certitudes upon which homophobia rests are subverted by this way of speaking.

In fact, the celebration of confusion embodied by such children's theories may be a more effective, interesting and radical way to enter gender politics than either the suspiciousness and judgementalism of the therapist or the nostalgia-fuelled return to certainty we see in some aspects of the men's movement or the advocacy of an ersatz merger of men's sociopolitical interests with those of women. Gender confusion unsettles all the main alternatives on offer.

What, then, does it mean that men are now increasingly seen as the problem? This new stance reverses the trend of centuries in which women – the other sex, the second sex, the dark sex, the sex which is not one – have been the problem men set themselves to solve. Nowadays, it is the men – sexually abusing, domestically violent, planet-despoiling creatures – who are depicted as the source of women's difficulties. There is little doubt that the accusation is valid. But a completely different set of images has also arisen, suggesting a breed of men who support the rights of women and children and are ecologically aware and non-violent. So we are faced with a split in our collective image of men. Conventionally, psychotherapists tell us that such splits come about when something (such as gender confusion) causes unbearable anxiety. It seems more likely that immense collective cultural anxiety is actually being caused by the false certitude of masculinity itself – what might be called 'the male deal'. It is the male deal that lies behind the deeply problematic gender certainty mentioned earlier. And it is the male deal that grounds our culture's assumptions about religion, science – and politics.

In the male deal, the little boy, at around the age of 3 or 4, strikes a bargain with the social world in which he lives. If he will turn away from soft things, feminine things, maternal things, from the world of play wherein failure does not matter, then the world will reward his gender certainty by giving him all the goodies in its possession – all the women he can eat. In return for the gift of political power, he promises to be a good provider and to keep unruly and subversive women and children in their place. He also promises not to deviate from this function by loving other men too much (that is, becoming gay). Homophobia is a political defence of the family as capitalism has defined it.

The question is whether or not we can reframe the collective confusion about the male deal as an opportunity to rethink a number of things: the deal itself and its damaging as well as pleasurable effects on men; the nature of male authority and its roots in Western attitudes to work; the possibility of women and men facing the difficult economic times ahead as partners as well as (not instead of) adversaries.

Given that men control the sources of economic and political power, including the production of ideas and images of sexual difference, then if men are on the move at some level, adding male political power to the ideals of male change could be decisive. In other words, we could be confronted with a social movement as significant as feminism but with the crucial difference that men are fortified with possession of all the resources from which women have been excluded.

Nothing is more suspect than the complaint, fuelled by

44

'victim envy', that society now favours women over men. Nevertheless, as suggested earlier, it would be wrong to end by reasserting that males have all the power. Perhaps there isn't a monolith called 'men' after all. As a woman in one of the workshops said of her husband: 'Well, if you take 1–5 and put it on one side and if you take 6–10 and put it on the other side – *he's in the abyss.*'

CHAPTER FOUR

The secret politics of the internal family

Is there a way to establish effective temporary new deals leading to alliances between women and men, accepting that there are ambivalent feelings between them? Can it be done without simplistic turnings to other cultures or other times in our own history as sources of inspiration? It should be possible, if we turn to 'the internal family' as it functions in each of us *now*. The internal family is not a universal and historically constant form or organization. The family has a changing social history. But everyone living in a given culture has a family inside his or her head, and that subjective, imaginal family is what is being depicted here. The internal family derives from one's own family as well as from images of 'family' which one has internalized.

There are four male–female relationships within the internal family which will be explored in turn: the mother–father relationship, the son–mother relationship, the daughter–father relationship and the brother–sister relationship. Thinking about these relationships will suggest templates, models and frameworks for progressive political alliances between women and men. (In Chapter 5, we shall explore the politics of relationships between the male figures of the internal family.)

46

THE SECRET POLITICS OF THE PARENTS IN BED

Let us now look at the *mother–father relationship* as a source of inspiration for thinking about the politics of women and men. If the personal is political, then there must be ways of taking personal, private psychological material and moulding, massaging, shaping it into something that has a political flavour.

Psychotherapists refer to the sexual act in your mind's eye between father and mother, between the man and woman who created you, as the 'primal scene'. The primal scene is a mixture of memory and fantasy elaborated over a lifetime that comes to symbolize everything about the relationship of your parents. As you read these words, think about the sex act that created you, about the intimate relationship of your parents or, if you grew up in a lone-parent family, of the sexual life of the parent with whom you grew up. What are its characteristics? What is the image that comes to mind? What are the emotional themes of *your* primal scene? Is it harmonious? Is it vigorous? Is there a sharing of power, or is there an imbalance? Is the bedroom door closed to you? These typical primal scene themes constitute the politics of the internal family. Think of the child's sense of exclusion – and then think of political discourse about marginal, dispossessed and excluded groups in society. Children are usually extremely curious about the sex life of their parents – it is the first investigative journalism or detective work any of us do. How much freedom of information was there about your parents' sexuality? Then there is the question of who initiates and who is setting the agenda of sexual behaviour – who is writing the manifesto and policy documents.

The political nature of the primal scene is illustrated by

the story of Lilith. The Midrash tells us that before Eve there was Lilith. God created Adam and Lilith from the same dust. On their first night in the garden, Adam mounts her, to have sex with her. She says: 'Get off me. Because why should you lie on top of me in the superior position when we were made at the same time, from the same stuff?' He rapes her. She cries out God's name, is drawn up into the stratosphere and then enjoys a subsequent career as the stereotypical she-demon, responsible for stillbirths on the one hand and wet dreams on the other, thereby becoming an emblem of that which most destabilizes traditional images of women (stillbirth) and traditional images of men (wet dreams, when the man loses control of his sexuality). This story is the politicized version of the primal scene. Not Adam and Eve, but Adam and Lilith and the politics of marital rape.

The imagery that people have within themselves of their parents' intimate life and sexual relationship is a general indicator of their politicality, political style and political values, their desire and capacity to do politics. The emotional tone of the primal scene moves between conflict and harmony, harmony and conflict. In particular, it is about enjoying enough conflict, enough sense of vigorous movement, to achieve a harmonious result, such as mutual sexual satisfaction and/or a baby. This can be seen as an analogy for the political process itself.

This survey of the politics of the internal family begins with the primal scene because it demonstrates how sexuality and politics symbolize each other, co-symbolize. The imagery that people have in their hearts and their mind's eye of their parents' sexual relationship tells them quite a lot, not only about their parents' relationship as they perceived it but also about their political selfhood, provided they decode it that way. It is a self-administered diagnostic test of people's political world views to dwell on this image of the most secret and intimate act that actually is responsible for their creation.

The experience of primal scene imagery may be additionally understood as expressing individuals' psychological approach to political functioning. The person's diverse psychic elements and agencies are coupled together into a unified whole *without* losing their separate identity – it is the great conundrum of universalism versus multiculturalism on the psychological level. Hence the image of the parents in bed depicts an unconscious engagement by the citizen with political problems that involve warring groups which cannot be reconciled. Mother and father are often at odds, quite different from each other – yet reconciliation is found in the primal scene. Similarly, commitment to reconciling opposites such as 'whites' and 'Blacks', Israelis and Palestinians, Catholics and Protestants, or rich and poor finds expression in parental imagery. Via primal scene imagery, the psyche is expressing citizens' capacity to cope with the unity *and* the diversity of the political situation they are in. As Aristotle said, 'Similars do not a state make.'

A further reason that the primal scene is so important for politics is that it invites us to address the conventional association of man with active and woman with passive sexual behaviour. This association both reflects and inspires many gender divisions. When individuals reflect on their primal scene imagery, it is remarkable that the conventional male-active/female-passive divide does *not* invariably appear. Quite the reverse. In fact, it often seems as if the unconscious 'intention' of the sexual imagery associated with the primal scene is to challenge that particular definition of the differences between men and women. The challenge to the sexual status quo symbolizes a kind of secret challenge to the political status quo. From the standpoint of gender politics, this enables us to introduce the mother in a transmogrified and politicized form: as an active player in the sexual game, and hence, potentially, as an active player in the political game.

The reproductive heterosexuality of the primal scene does not necessarily exclude people of homosexual sexual orientation. The fruitfulness signified in the primal scene, and the problems therein, are completely congruent with homosexual experience. But there is a set of cultural and intellectual assumptions that needs to be explicated. Why is it that psychological fecundity, variety and liveliness do not yet get imaged or theorized in homosexual terms? Why is psychological maturity still envisaged in a form of complementary wholeness that requires heterosexual imagery for it to work at all? One could easily defend the thesis that heterosexual primal scene imagery works quite happily for persons of homosexual orientation by recourse to metaphor, saying that primal scene heterosexuality refers, not to the fact of reproduction, but to heterosexual intercourse as a symbol of diversity, otherness, conflict, potential. Similarly, one could also point out that, since everyone is the result of a heterosexual union, heterosexual symbolism is simply inevitable and not excluding of a homosexual orientation.

I am dubious about these liberal manoeuvres because they still leave a question mark in my mind concerning the absence of texts *replete with homosexual imagery that would perform the psychological and political functions of primal scene imagery*. We might begin a search for the homosexual primal scene. Though this idea sounds controversial, it merely involves a recognition that the primal scene is about political processes and not only about the personal parents.

Personal narratives of primal scene imagery, and their working through, demonstrate to a considerable extent a person's capacity to sustain political conflict constructively. But what of the missing primal scene, the well-known problem of *not being able to imagine the parents' sex life at all*, or of having a bland and non-erotic image of it? Clearly, denial and repression play an important role, but there seems to be more than just personal ego-defence mechanisms involved. This non-primal scene derives in the first instance from a colossal fear of the consequences of conflict. (Again, *sexual* conflict co-symbolizing *political* conflict.) For if the bodies of the parents are not in motion, then psychological and sociopolitical differences and inequalities between male and female need not enter consciousness. The denied primal scene signifies a loss of faith in the political nature of the human organism and of society itself. Conversely, images of vigorous, mutually satisfying parental intercourse – including, perhaps, some kind of struggle for power – reveal a private engagement with the conflictual political dynamics of the public sphere.

In workshops on transformative politics, I ask participants to divide a sheet of paper vertically. In the left-hand column, they are to list (a) their earliest memory (or notion of their earliest memory) of their parents' physical intimacy; (b) the same at adolescence; (c) the same today. In the right-hand column, they should list (a) their earliest political memory or the first time they became aware of a situation of political conflict; (b) their politics at adolescence and their general attitude to politics at that time; (c) the same today. The participants are asked to take home the piece of paper with its two columns – primal scene and politics. All they are asked to do is to reflect on what they have written, scanning the entries in the two columns referring to each point in time and the developmental process revealed by a comparison of the two columns.

Here is an example of what one participant in the exercise wrote together with a comment by him. He was 47 years old at the time, married with one child and working in publishing.

Earliest memory of parents

Seeing mother lying on her back, head propped up. Father on his side with one arm across her breasts, in my association, in a supplicant role.

My earliest political memory

Suez. Talk of the end of Britain as a strong country. Demonization of Nasser.

Parents at adolescence

False relationship put on for others. Like a historical posed portrait, arm-in-arm but stiff and formal.

My politics at adolescence

Total revolution. Idealism. Lots of energy. Love of action, even of violence.

Parental relationship today

Mother dominant due to father's age and infirmity. A lot of togetherness. Anxiety, clinging together like babes in wood.

My politics today

Sadness at state of world and cynicism of politicians. Anger at young people who do not organize enough. Fascinated by earth-based social action movements.

Comment: I had a lot of trouble even thinking about this. I had not heard of the primal scene before. I can see how my parents' marriage has affected my own family life because I am very careful not to be dominated. You seem to be asking me to tell you something that I did not know I knew but I can see that there are crossovers between the parents and my politics such as they are. The weak father and weak Britain. My idealism as an adolescent compared to their falseness. Sadness at politics today and sadness at my parents' anxious state.

THE SECRET POLITICS OF SONS AND MOTHERS

Conventional psychological accounts of the *son–mother relationship* address the son like this:

> You must separate from your mother lest you fall into a female identification. Your mother is dangerous, seductive and engulfing. You must not be a mother's boy. You must give up mother to father. You must give up mother to siblings. You must give up mother to her own destiny.

The implied message in all this is:

> You must harden yourself against the feminine. You'd better follow soccer. Take a stand against softness. Reject notions of play, imagination and relatedness. You may not grow in connection.

But do males really have to separate from their mothers – their 'suffocating', 'possessive', 'Jewish', 'Mediterranean' mothers – as the books say they must? Do they have to *slay* the maternal monster? Do they have to be that kind of hero? Is this the only valid path of ego development? Or is it possible to get beyond a situation where the son is required always to be an active, heroic and somewhat disengaged man, and the mother is always depicted as a swampy, seductive maternal monster who is full of feelings? Unfortunately, as Jung pointed out,

> the heroic deed of slaying the maternal monster has no lasting effects. Again and again, the hero must renew the struggle and always under the symbol of deliverance from the mother. Just as Hera, in her role of the pursuing mother, is the source of the mighty deeds performed by Herakles, so Nacomis allows Hiawatha no rest but piles up new difficulties in his path. The mother is thus the Daemon who challenges the hero to his deeds and lays in his path the poisonous serpent that will strike him.[1]

But what if we were to recognize that both son and mother want to separate? What if this were the progressive *political* element in the psychological experience of maternal ambivalence, which, as Roszika Parker has suggested, aids creative maternal thought?[2] Is the image of St George slaying the Dragon, which is the underlying cultural image behind Western science as the boy scientist dissects Mother Nature, the only basis upon which science can proceed? What has been called a feminization of science is taking place, whereby the epistemological relations between the exploring ego and its subject matter are being completely reframed. These feminist-inspired new approaches to science parallel a less adversarial reframing of the son–mother relationship.[3]

Traditionally, the theological and psychological question has been how to extract spirit (intellect, autonomy) out of the earthy mother's body and preserve it. What about extracting the *politics* from her relationship with her son? What would maternal leadership look like? Could a new version of the son–mother relationship provide a more realistic basis for what is involved in the New Man phenomenon? If there is going to be a new relationship of men to the environment to set alongside ecofeminism, doesn't there have to be a new reading of the son–mother relationship? The symbolic connection of earth and mother is not necessarily demeaning to mothers.

Regarding political behaviour, might the politics of protection and nurture be practised by others beside mothers?[4] We could identify a kind of politics based on and symbolized by the caring labour of mothers that might lead us to discover more about the caring labour of sons, including to what extent *sons* could care for sick and elderly people, and involving models of nursing and teaching appropriate for *sons*. An important spin-off would be adequate levels of pay for the 'caring professions'. Son–mother inspired political behaviour would certainly involve nurture and imagination. This would be a style of politics that struggles to eschew or give up conventional power, performing an anti-heroic move in relation to politics.

The son–mother connection might be re-read as radical, friendly to males and fair. There is some danger of idealizing the mother in this. But as we cannot just *stop* seeing mother as swamp, the danger is not great; there will always be a fearsome maternal element to consider. In any case, there is more than just idealization of the mother going on here. Changes in social and political practices are taking place right now (nurturing fathers, brotherly men, male politicians who speak as men) that put pressure on the established order to change.

One implication of re-reading the mother–son relationship is a reversal in trend of nearly all psychological approaches to politics, in which the citizen is seen primarily as

a child and even, if the viewpoint is psychoanalytic, as a baby.
Then the child-citizen is up against a parental society. (One
British example would be Mrs Thatcher as the citizenry's
mother.) But why can't the citizen of whatever sex and age be
a mother to society? The usual positioning of the citizen as a
child is extremely destructive to transformative politics. It
represents the collusion of psychoanalysis with the interests
of the powerful, who have an investment in keeping citizens
as children. We can start to think about the citizen as an
adult, and specifically as a mother. Each citizen can take a
maternal attitude towards the social issues and social problems in the culture that she or he inhabits. For example, the
maternal viewpoint would tend to foreground health issues
(physical and mental). Policy decisions to do with transport,
defence, education would be addressed primarily from the
point of view of their impact on health.

A maternal approach to politics could also radicalize economic thinking. Economists talk about exchange value, by
which they mean the money/price value of things. However
sentimental it may sound, there is also 'emotional value' to
consider. What are the emotional consequences of such and
such an economic decision – to build a motorway, to build a
nuclear submarine, to raise or lower income tax? What are
the consequences for the emotional life of the nation? There
are also aesthetic ramifications to consider. What are the aesthetic consequences of policy decisions? Do they add to or
subtract from the store of beauty in a society? (These questions are taken up in more detail in Chapter 9.)

Pulling it all together, if we start to think again about the
mother–son relationship, and stop seeing these two as life-
long enemies, it is possible to imagine the emergence of a
maternal approach to political behaviour that would, for

example, envision self-esteem and self-respect as distributable goods that can be fought over and contested in a society. Nurture, containment and care would become the highest political values in contradistinction to productivity and decisiveness.

THE SECRET POLITICS OF DAUGHTERS AND FATHERS

As far as the *daughter–father relationship* is concerned, something has gone awfully wrong with our world's response to the father's body. Alongside the problems of child sexual abuse, about which we now know a great deal, we should also recognize the opposite problem and speak out against the daughter–father relationship remaining stunted, inhibited and cool. The block may be to do with our reaction to the male body generally, but it is highlighted by our thinking concerning the father's body in relation to his daughter. In all the quite justifiable concern over child sexual abuse, we have forgotten that there are psychologically benevolent uses of the father's body in the emotional development of children of both sexes. Here, I discuss fathers and daughters; in Chapter 5, fathers and sons.

'Erotic playback' from father to daughter communicates to her that she need not be restricted to the role of mother. The bodily warmth of erotic playback involves an admiring communication of the daughter's sexual viability that does not lead to any kind of physical enactment. Psychotherapists hear about fathers who have failed to deliver erotic playback to their daughters – a positive message carried by the erotic dimension of their relationship that she is something other than a maternal creature who puts the needs of others first. Deficits in erotic playback can lead to serious psychological problems that are still overlooked by many therapists. It is extremely difficult to get this issue discussed without being accused of advocating incest.

But what is the connection of erotic playback to political behaviour? Breaking up the equation 'woman equals mother' leads to the possibility of other pathways for female development – pathways of spiritual development, self-assertion, vocation and even unrelated sex and lust. (The last is something men know more about as a pathway of development. It is not the only way to function, and certainly not the most elevated way, but it is *a* way.) Then there are pathways that have nothing to do with men at all: community and solidarity with other women that may or may not involve lesbianism, or celibacy. Once we break up a rigid equation that has too much gender certainty in it, we open up the doorways to other possible kinds of relationship. This is what may be very hard to accept: that paternal sexuality has this door-opening function.

There is also an important contribution to be made here to what has been called 'the politics of time': how a woman organizes her life, how she copes with the balancing act or juggling act between the various selves that she inhabits. Erotic playback cannot solve the highly charged problem of the politics of time central in the lives of many women (which is also becoming much more important for men). But it plays a part in contributing to a person's capacity to think about it.

What about the father's aggression? Is that always a negative factor? On the contrary, the way he deploys, uses and inhabits his own body serves to communicate to his daughter that it is OK to be angry. The father's body as a forum, a place in which father and daughter can practise and experiment with different styles of aggression. *Mouth aggression* – verbal onslaughts. *Leg and foot aggression* – when each walks away from the other. *Genital aggression* – a disparaging of the sexual beauty of the other. *Anal aggression* – a smearing, envious, mocking kind of attack. It is important not to get stuck in one style or mode of aggression and to become competent at rotating through a plurality of aggressions.

The argument is social and political as well as psychological; the idea of erotic playback and aggressive playback does not apply only to male fathers. In Chapter 7, I explain why I decided to coin the phrase 'the good-enough father of whatever sex'. Research work with lone-parent families had shown that, while women parenting alone (or together with other women) may not do things in quite the same way that men do them, that does not mean there is inevitably a psychological deficit. Certainly, the reverse is true: there are numerous people who had two parents and grew up in a conventional family who are very unhappy.

THE SECRET POLITICS OF BROTHERS
AND SISTERS

Finally, we come to the *brother–sister relationship*. Many psychological texts about sisters and brothers seem intent on establishing the unsavoury and harmful aspects of this relationship in spite of the fact that many people have enjoyed their siblings enormously. The focus is on rivalry or on the different projections siblings receive from their parents. Jealousy and over-involvement with each other feature prominently with physical incest as a threatening spectre. When adulthood is attained, the sibling relationship receives a tangential putdown – sibling-style marriage is stated to be a bad thing. Marriages go wrong when there is too much of a brother–sister tone to them.

This relationship is certainly different from marriage or romantic love, which is precisely why I want to celebrate it as the repository of a great deal of secret political energy. We can think, for example, of the political significance of the story of Antigone and her opposition to the forces of law and tradition motivated by loyalty to and love of her brother.

The sister–brother relationship provides us with an extremely useful image for addressing a key political problem in liberal societies. We are all *supposed* to be equal, but in fact we are not. Similarly, the brother–sister relationship in modern Western societies is supposed to be a relationship of equals within the family. It can be, but it often is not. Hence it is absolutely full of politically suggestive ambivalence. How do brothers and sisters relate politically? What do they do that we could get some political juice out of?

When the first sibling reaches the age of 11 or 12, something repressive happens to the sister–brother connection. They stop talking. They start mocking, or they become silent and withdrawn from each other. The conventional explanation is that this has to do with sex. Clearly, puberty is relevant. But there is also something else going on. At 11 or 12 years, a child is a real, actual and even physical threat to parental authority. To the degree that parental authority carries the state's authority, it is crucial for the preservation of the state's authority (as well as the parents' authority) that the generational bonding of the sister–brother relationship remain politically depotentiated. When culture smashes the psychological structure of seduction between siblings, it also smashes the political structure of resistance or allows a less potent form to exist – for example, when an older sibling protects a younger one against parental maltreatment; this is rather different from an active alliance of siblings.

There is a 'natural' political struggle involving children versus parents within the family that we need to know more about. It is a struggle for social justice based on the struggle between the generations of a family, whether a family in the social world or an internal family of the inner world. The psychological linkage between family and society needs fleshing out. As far as social reform is concerned, perhaps things change so slowly and with such difficulty because we have depoliticized and depotentiated the sibling relationship in families, which makes it very difficult to establish it or re-establish it in societies. This would politically explain the psychological aspects of the worldwide attack on trade unions. Whether we call it fraternity or sisterhood or sibling politics, it is feared by those in power and hence not wanted. Sibling politics is far too threatening to conventional ideas of good order (and leadership) in the political realm.

It is often hard to get a discussion going about the in-eluctable, unavoidable, unhealable but potentially radical ambivalence between the sexes. The brother–sister story is a useful and interesting way to start to address the theme, of-fering the possibility that men and women can do their politics as men and as women, which is what many if not most of them want to do. Ambivalence, perhaps the most difficult thing to manage in political as well as in psychological terms, is written into the sibling relationship just as it is written into social relations generally.

The brother–sister relationship may also be seen as a

metaphor for approaches to politics arising from information technology and the Internet, with the focus on exchanges of information. Here, one thinks of the ideals behind the Internet, rather than its inevitable, disappointing fate as part of someone's media empire. Such ideals include mutual learning, a non-hierarchical approach to communication and a respect for indigenous knowledge. These are also the secret ideals of the brother–sister relationship, which we could consider factoring into attempts to construct a new kind of politics.

In other words, the original, close, playful brother–sister relationship – before it breaks down – can serve as a useful model for progressive political action as well as relations between the sexes. Political organization based on the brother–sister relationship will be less hierarchical and more co-operative. Or, to be realistic, factoring the brother–sister relationship into existing attempts to construct egalitarian political organizations might make these much more exciting to participate in than is often the case. For all its ambivalent, intricate complexities, the image of the brother–sister relationship brings a strong energic charge when aligned with political activity.

Yet instead of actively trying to promote such horizontal, co-operative relationships in the political sphere, our politicians and public figures usually call for the restoration and strengthening of the traditional vertical relationships that characterize formal politics. Surely what is needed is not greater verticality – more authority figures, more deference and obedience – but a horizontal politics that will lead to sibling justice and new deals between women and men, however temporary that may be. There will be interesting pay-offs for both sexes.

Men may get women to listen more closely to some of their concerns and worries, for example health concerns ranging from declining sperm counts to coronary disease and testicular cancer. Can women take these things seriously, not only on a personal but also on a collective, political level? Within a sibling mode of politics, they can.

Conversely, what would 'sisters' want to say that might get a hearing from 'brothers'? However useful the image of the goddess may have been to some women, by and large women have been ill-served by the kind of essentialist literature that insists that they be true, deep, pure, integrated, related, containing, nourishing, wild, earthy goddesses. Why should not women be allowed to lie, to be ingenious, to improvise, to deny reality, to move more confidently in public, urban places at all hours of the day and night, to mock the 'rules' that contain them, to play power games? The female Trickster that one can glimpse bubbling under the surface of Western cultures – like all Tricksters – cannot be praised for her depth and purity.

(In Chapter 6, siblings and Tricksters reappear in the context of political leadership and organization.)

CHAPTER FIVE

The secret psychology of political forms

WHERE DO new political ideas come from? How are they carried within a culture? How do they acquire form and spread? This chapter discusses several questions about political change, using relationships between men as the raw material. The common-sense or obvious answers to these questions are that political ideas spread by word of mouth, by people's (subversive) reading of texts, by spawning organizations and so forth. But there might be something else that a psychological approach can flesh out – a political *Zeitgeist*, a political spirit of the time, a secret life of politics.

POLITICAL FORMS

To clarify what is meant by 'political form': the reference is to units of understanding and action within a society that combine the effects of ideology, narratives of emotional experience and eventual organizational structure. I see such forms as having a purpose or goal, and also as having a much less tangible, more hermeneutic function. We talk about such things all the time when we talk about what kind of organization an institution or even a country is. We talk about an institution that is not a prison as if it were a prison. We talk about an institution that is not a madhouse as if it were a madhouse. We sometimes refer to places of work as families. A journalist might describe a corrupt corporation or government agency as a 'den of iniquity', though the bureaucratic, dry-as-dust organization being referred to could not be further from a 'den of iniquity'. What are we doing when we characterize organizations in this way? We are speaking a language of political forms. We have a gestaltic image of the political form: its appearance plus its character plus our evaluation of it, all held together at once. The idea is to add something psychological to a materialist version of the social.[1]

There are many uses of the term 'form' in other disciplines. In biology, form means a variant type of life, something to do with the morphology, the shape, the bodily character of an organism. In philosophy, the term can mean the essential character of something. In social theory, it means, loosely, organization. There are, if you trawl dictionary and thesaurus, some fascinating and suggestive additional meanings. Form can mean to train or develop something or someone. A form is a document with blank spaces to fill in.

There is something about social organisms that we cannot measure or assess accurately. The scientific fantasy breaks down. We cannot weigh a political form or describe political forms in minute, empirical detail. This is true of a factory, a university, or an economic system. Social organisms are very difficult to speak about with accuracy.

Another feature of form is that the same elements can lead to different forms. We learn this from biology, chemistry and sociology. Now, if the same elements lead to different forms, is there not something more than a material factor or set of factors to be considered? It is not a question of eternal Platonic forms, or what one might call political archetypes. Nor should one conclude, *qua* Aristotle, that there are particular political forms that are natural for political functions. Nor, clearly, is this a mechanistic perspective.

Perhaps political forms involve psychological fields which influence their creation, existence and, above all, mutability. It is still rather a mystery how political forms come into being and change over time. There is no 'egg', there are no 'genes', in most visions of the social. But there might be a place for a kind of 'social vitalism' based on psychology.

Vitalism holds that living organisms are organized by purposeful, mind-like principles. Teleology may be a dirty word these days, but even a materialist like Richard Dawkins uses its close neighbour, teleonomy, to link his Darwinism and the notion of final causes or purposes.[2] There may be a purposive organizing principle in the social, which creates and destroys political forms, both ones that we approve of and ones that we disapprove of. If this process is non-material in nature, then it will include human psychology.

INCESTUOUS SEXUAL FANTASY AND THE NEW POLITICAL FORMS

Which aspects of psychology are most suggestive in relation to political change? What about unconscious fantasies of incestuous sexuality that drive the psychological relationships within the internal family? Might these have some effect on the way in which political ideas form and spread? Examining these fantasies and relationships, and what we think about them, may help us to speculate more fruitfully about how political ideas are generated, how they are transmitted in a culture and, to borrow a phrase of Stuart Hall's, how they have been 'sleeping in the public language'.[3]

We usually approach incest in terms of pair relationships, despite the fact that family therapists have noted the existence of incestuous patterns, atmospheres and systems in families. But what holds these pairs together? According to Jung, the answer to that question is 'kinship libido', which, to use his phrase, is like 'a sheepdog keeping the family intact'.[4] A further question that might fruitfully be addressed concerns the role of kinship libido in society. Critically examined, can kinship libido be socialized, that is, understood in broad terms as holding social organisms and political forms together? If so, different facets of kinship libido, different kinds of incestuous sexual fantasies, will be involved in the emergence and destruction of different political forms. At one point, Jung hints that kinship libido helps to hold 'creeds, parties, nations or states together'.[5] Here we see an enormous difference from Freud, who, taking incest fantasy more literally and less metaphorically than Jung, identified the need to protect culture and civilization from the incestuous components of Eros.

A radical re-reading of the secret politics of highly charged relationships in the family can inspire new ideas about political forms, as well as helping us to analyse existing ones. To the extent that psychology has built itself around sexuality and gender, these aspects of relations between people in conventional and unconventional families are the viable way to factor the psychological dimension into political discourse.

The problem with this approach to political forms is that it courts danger because of the presence of incestuous sexual fantasy. However, it is precisely the transgressive nature of incestuous fantasy (to be distinguished from actual incest which is always destructive) that makes it a useful metaphor in developing transgressive politics.

SON–FATHER POLITICAL FORMS

Scanning basic introductory texts in psychotherapy, we see that the *son–father relationship* is said to involve sexual rivalry, castration, the figure of the absent father, the father as a role model for the son, the father as a law-giver for the son, the father as a moral presence, the father as either a success or a failure at separating the son from suffocating symbiosis with the mother.

The notion of benevolent erotic playback, this time between father and son not father and daughter, reframes the relationship in both bodily and political terms.[6] The father's body also becomes a forum in which son and father work together on the transformation of aggression in its destructive and antisocial forms into a more socially creative kind of self-assertion. Aggression can never be eliminated as such, but the movements within the aggressive process can be tracked.

Because erotic playback contains elements of admiration and even longing and yearning for the son, it is also empowering for the son, and leads to 'homosociality'. (This term, suggested to me by Sonu Shamdasani, is one that Eve Kosofsky Sedgwick first used in a different context.[7]) Homosociality can be illustrated concretely by the way in which the gay

68

community has responded to the challenge of HIV/AIDS, particularly when HIV/AIDS was thought to be an exclusively homosexual problem. So homosociality is already involved in a reframing of what many want from contemporary political organizations. But there is more to homosociality than loving co-operation between men of different generations. Homosociality inspires a covenant of mutual protection between father and son in which they agree to look after, take care of, speak for, and protect the human rights of the other. However, in order for this covenant to come alive, father and son have to overcome the homosexual inhibition that our culture has placed so firmly at the heart of male identity. Overcoming the homosexual inhibition moves us towards an apprehension of what male nurturing might look like, and that itself constitutes an enormous challenge to most conventionally accepted ideas about the son–father relationship.

As regards the new political forms that might stem from this relationship, and the challenge that they mount to conventional ways of doing things, the most important element is co-operation based on homosociality derived from erotic playback. Father–son co-operation based on a covenant forged in the heat of their bodily interaction and communication – hence involving incestuous sexual fantasy – is primarily about non-hierarchical relating *between* males rather than two males relating together to an external object, such as football, or against a perceived threat, such as women. The move from boyhood to manhood involves more than an evolving recognition that one is not female. Father–son relating provides a practical and inspiring political model. Love between them is a kind of political practice.

One thing to note here is the absence in our culture of

much gay/straight dialogue about these things. Gay men know about giving and receiving bodily affirmation within an eroticized, loving context. Heterosexual men know less about it and there is a potentially very important political and psychological dialogue to consider. Notice the paradox: the group of men regarded by our society as the least 'manly' can be re-imagined as pioneers, frontiersmen and the leaders of a different kind of politics.

Most fathers want to be directly involved with their children and to have a passionate, intense, responsible relationship with them. The biggest obstacle is that such aspirations bring up the fear of effeminacy. And effeminacy, in our world, brings up the spectre of homosexuality, because male homosexuals are not proper men (and hence must surely be women). If male homosexuals are really women, then the usual male fear and loathing of femininity also kick in. If new political forms are to come into being that could make use of the energies in new images of nurturing fathers, we will have to come to grips with our enormous fear of softness, effeminacy and hence, by association, of homosexuality. (Psychoanalysis in particular needs to consider the prejudicial tendency in the theory that considers male homosexuals to be female- or mother-identified.)

The male body has received political attention mainly as a destructive presence in society. However, the supposed vulnerability of the male body, exemplified in the relatively new emphasis on men's health issues, may be an important plank in the construction of homosocial political forms. Male physical vulnerability is a contemporary form of male hysteria perhaps, less real than apparent, and mimetically linked to the roles of victim, underdog and abused one. Hence it is imitative of women and children. It should not be allowed to obscure the sociopolitical realities of male power often mobilized in support of 'traditional' family roles. As Lynne Segal has shown, the very existence of a homogeneous entity called 'men' is extremely dubious.[8] Yet the images of vulnerable men with which we are confronted nowadays bear a political significance that cannot be easily dismissed.

BROTHER–BROTHER POLITICAL FORMS

The second all-male relationship in the internal family is the *brother–brother relationship*. The conventional depiction of the brother–brother relationship is extraordinarily pathological. Nobody denies that it is a very important relationship; everyone refers to Cain and Abel or Jacob and Esau – but there is rarely any mention of the team of Moses and Aaron (who did Moses' talking for him). The general consensus seems to be that there is something a bit odd about too good a brotherly relationship. Fraternity is closely linked to pathology in psychoanalysis. Most writers seem to be comfortable discussing the brother–brother relationship in terms of rivalry, or depicting the brothers as receiving very opposite parental projections – if one is made into the thinker, then the other will be made into the doer. There is even a strand of imagery in the psychotherapy literature that suggests that the collective psychoanalytic association to brotherhood is rather bestial: we hear about top dogs, bottom dogs and runts of litters. Finally, most texts on the brother relation do not stay with its particularity but move rapidly on to position the brothers in relation to the father (primal horde thinking).

My critique of this thinking is that psychotherapists have

encouraged our culture to pathologize away a particular kind of political connection between men. This has been done by equating psychic growth and psychic health with absorption of the other, integration of the opposite, the whole hetero-thing. We need to discuss whether health, or maturity, or growth always has to be in relation to something that is 'other'. The notion that we develop solely or mainly by absorbing or relating to or getting into a 'marriage' with the other is one we get from society and culture, but therapists have also promoted it. As is so often the case, they both reflect the prejudices of their culture and contribute to those prejudices. Hence, if psychic health and growth and thus social health and growth are predicated on absorption of the other, the brother–brother relation and brotherliness are ruled out of court as sources of health on grounds of excessive similarity.

Perhaps it is time to resurrect the notion of the soulmate, but within an all-male frame. We can think of the social aspects of warmth and closeness between men, homosexual as well as homosocial, in terms of the particular psychology of the double. Psychological and social growth rest on an encounter with the double. In Sumerian myth, we find the tale of the relationship between Gilgamesh and Enkidu, who appear in each other's dreams and also swap roles; each of them takes on the bloodthirsty and out-of-control role and also the rational role in turn. This kind of metaphorical *brotherliness* needs to be distinguished from *brotherhoods* – the army, the locker room, the college fraternity, the old boys' network, the Masons, the Broederbund, the secret society. Such well-known misogynistic bastions of male solidarity and power can be usefully understood as disavowals of or flights from the all-but-homosexual social and personal brotherly aspects of the brother pair. The role of the brother–brother relationship in male friendship patterns, and hence its potential to lead to fraternal political organization as a whole, is a topic about which very little has been written, although one meets with numerous spontaneous references to David and Jonathan (not biological brothers). This contrasts with sisterliness and its ubiquitous role in female friendship and the sociopolitical organization of women. Apollo and Hermes are a further positive example: sibling gods who function as the missing bit of each other. This is symbolized by the way they resolve their dispute over Hermes' theft of Apollo's cattle: an exchange of gifts whereby Hermes gives Apollo his lyre, making him the god of music, and Apollo gives Hermes the cattle.

What would new political forms inspired by brotherliness look like? What do we find if we analyse today's political forms with these thoughts about the brother–brother relationship in mind? For many reasons, there is a huge contemporary silence on the subject of fraternity. We still talk about liberty, and equality is continuously discussed. But fraternity has gone missing. The calamitous decline of trade unions is a significant feature here, illustrating the ways in which fraternity and political forms inspired by fraternity have slipped off the agenda. We are enmeshed in the politics of leadership and the models for leadership that we have inherited are paternal and heroic models with little place for the brotherly double.

The political translation of these ideas about the brother–brother relationship promotes a different model of political leadership. What would fraternal (or sibling) leadership look like? This is difficult to answer (though I attempt it in Chapter 6) because most of us have little experience of such a paradoxical political form. It has not been much theorized. One example of leadership in a sibling vein occurs at meetings of witches' covens – Wiccan groups. Men can attend such covens. At a meeting of a coven that I attended, use was made of a 'speaking stick'. When a speaker had finished, she or he passed a staff to the person they had chosen to speak next. This replaced the more adversarial pattern of conventional political meetings. Differences of opinion were introduced gradually and, over time, everyone present got to speak, but within a different structure – or form – of communication.

CHAPTER SIX

The good-enough leader

A S STATED in the opening chapters, psychotherapists and analysts have always wanted to explore the social world and current events. It is not a new fad or fashion. Freud hoped to understand 'the riddles of the world', and Jung said that therapists 'cannot avoid coming to grips with contemporary history'.[1] But, as we saw, many attempts to link psychotherapy and social issues have tended to present everything as exclusively psychological, thereby keeping the therapist in control and above the fray. In particular, attempts to put political leaders and other significant figures such as Bill Clinton, Tony Blair or Princess Diana on the couch as patients have, quite rightly, been criticized and ridiculed.

It is crucial not to confuse or conflate the processes that go on within an individual with what happens on the much more complex level of society. The basic claim of this book is that, provided such errors are avoided, psychotherapy can be a useful and imaginative tool of social criticism rather than descending into self-indulgent psycho-babble. The temptation to analyse prominent people in public should be resisted and, instead, fruitful working partnerships can be forged with people working in social policy, education, the media and environmentalism. Therapists and analysts also need to recall that not everything is rosy in their own professional politics; they must avoid giving the impression that they have all the answers.

Having indicated that it is not my intention to analyse specific leaders, in the spirit of ground clearing let me indicate some other angles on leadership that will *not* be pursued. The familiar debate over whether leaders are more likely to be exceptional individuals in themselves or simply the persons of the moment will not be revisited. Nor is a list going to be provided of the psychological attributes of a successful leader, which is the kind of empirical project often carried out by academic political psychology.[2]

In contradistinction to many psychological commentators on politics, I will not be exploring the motivations of citizens who follow individuals leading large movements or parties. The chapter is not about crowd psychology or large group dynamics. Although the word 'power' cannot be avoided in relation to leadership, whether in its benevolent or malevolent aspects, the chapter is not a study in power. Nor does it very much concern the ubiquitous, impersonal forces of, for example, globalization or international finance, which contribute so much to the intractability of many social issues and problems. Nor will the focus be on what we as citizens might do when faced with the collapse of much we had previously taken for granted in the world of politics. The aim is to advance an image-based, hence psychological approach to leadership itself.

One final introductory point: quite a lot of what might sound like *advocacy* in this chapter is in fact *description*. Intellectuals have learned over the years that much high-powered theorizing is often nothing more than an excellent description of cutting-edge practice. What seems to be a contribution to thinking about leadership probably reflects what is going on in practice already. Insights arise from new political forms that were already there, hidden in the open. For example, Machiavelli did not actually advocate what successful princes should do in sixteenth-century Italy. Rather, he can now be seen to have described the actions of the most successful princes of his day. But he was the one who brought the issue into cultural consciousness, forming it into a discourse. Similarly, Adam Smith was not advocating what capitalists should do at the end of the eighteenth century. He was merely describing what the new entrepreneurs and financial manipulators were already doing.

GOOD-ENOUGHNESS

Many readers will know that the British psychoanalyst Donald Winnicott coined the phrase 'the good-enough mother' (although nowadays people tend to talk about 'the good-enough parent'). Winnicott meant that, after a period in which parents do their best to meet the omnipotent fantasies and expectations of the baby, there comes a recognition that the 'perfect fit' is not going to work psychologically or behaviourally for either party. What ensues, at least in Western families, is a kind of graduated let-down or disappointment of the baby carried out by her or his parents. The baby is carefully introduced to the realities of life, in which one cannot expect omnipotently determined, magical, hyper-pleasurable satisfaction of instinctual needs. Included is the difficult-to-bear realization that no one is self-created.

How does a parent make the move from being the perfect

parent of omnipotent fantasy to becoming the good-enough parent? One key way in which parents become good-enough facilitators of their babies' development is by *failing their babies*. At the heart of good-enoughness lies a certain kind of failure. It is this particular aspect of good-enoughness that I want to detach carefully from the world of developmental psychology, from fleshly family life, in order to see whether the notion of good-enoughness does have a utility in relation to politics in general and to the issue of leadership in particular. We are talking not only about the art of parenting, but also about the art of politics when we identify a middle way that steers a course between idealizing the parents (or leaders) on the one hand and denigrating them on the other. Please note: the suggestion is not that leaders are parents – only that, if we want to avoid the extremes of idealization and denigration in relation to leaders, the qualities and processes that go into good-enough parenthood are equally pertinent to good-enough leadership. The issue is whether we can pick our way between the *idealizations* of leaders that we see all too often in extreme form in the quietistic acceptance of despotic, fascistic and tyrannical leaders, and today's equally striking *denigrations*, with nobody trusting anyone in a position of authority. The issues Winnicott highlighted – the move away from idealization and denigration, the introduction of a dose of realism in a graduated and manageable way, the enabling of the child to become more active, autonomous and self-reliant as a by-product of parental failure – are highly relevant to the political situation in many Western countries. Failure, with accompanying feelings of being let down and disappointed, is an inevitability. Yet our political vocabulary seems less than adequate to address this. Hence the borrowing of the notion of good-enoughness is suggestive of ways of coping with political disappointments without excessive dependence on a tyrannical leader on the one hand or exasperated and disgusted withdrawal from the political process on the other. If our goal is perfection, we are doomed to subside into despair and depression; we feel impotent and cannot act. If we only see how awful everything is, we are tempted to wash our hands of politics and let others (leaders) deal with things; we are paralysed and, again, lose our sense of agency.

LEADERSHIP AND FAILURE

Failure is a core element of good-enoughness. The linkages between the idea of failure and the question of good-enough leadership include (a) failed leaders, (b) the failure in our time of the very idea of leadership, and (c) leadership as the study and practice of failure – leadership as the art of failing. (This division incorporates some of the features of James Hillman's study of failure in clinical analysis.[3]) As Bob Dylan put it, 'There's no success like failure, and failure's no success at all.'

The first occasion on which I raised the issue of the intimate linkages between leadership and failure was at the annual Congress of the British Labour Party in 1994. The reaction should probably not have seemed as startling as it did. There was serious and lively TV, radio and press coverage of what was received as a fresh idea that the image of failure could stimulate discussions of the nature of leadership. Vehement responses suggested that placing leadership, failure and good-enoughness in the same frame took some kind of shackles off people's political imaginations.

As far as *failed leaders* are concerned, it seems that those leaders commonly agreed by political historians to have failed have mostly been either falsely strong figures or, conversely, manifestly weak, indecisive ones – devoted to pleasing others and hence unable to do whatever they were supposed to do. Academic and biographical studies of leaders also suggest that failed leaders often have a great capacity for self-deception. The most famous example is, of course, Hitler, who in 1945 was busy moving non-existent armies around the map of Europe as Berlin crumbled about him.

A further aspect of failed leaders is that their styles of leadership are just plain wrong for the time they are in. The way that some individuals want to lead, a way that seems 'natural' to them, does not seem to fit with what the populace is willing to accept.

Riding your luck seems to be very important for successful leaders. Machiavelli wrote beautifully about this. One of the main things a prince needs to be able to do is to make use of *fortuna* – by which he meant more than luck: *fortuna* involves elements of alignment and harmony with the rhythms of the universe. But the modern notion of luck is by no means a trivial concept, especially when considered with leadership in mind, and especially when the stakes are at the life-and-death level.

We move on now to consider the second connection between leadership and failure: *the failure, in our time, of the very idea of leadership*. We are in a strikingly split situation over this whole question of leadership. Our cognitive understanding of the way in which received ideas about strong and successful leaders have failed us has got far ahead of our emotional capacity to manage the realization that, as Brecht has Galileo put it, 'Unhappy is the country that needs a hero.'

By now, everybody knows that apparently strong and manifestly heroic leaders are deeply suspect. They are hyper-masculine or macho personages, and, intellectually speaking, we don't want them. They are 'male' whatever their actual sex because, for heroes, the obstacles to be overcome are, in Western discourse, always 'female'. They are dangerous, whether they are playing the role of saviour, explorer, king, philosopher or warrior. And in the nuclear age in which we continue to live, it is quite clear why they are dangerous. Everybody knows this on an intellectual level. Women know it, for sure. All over the world, women are deeply suspicious of male and, indeed, female heroic leaders and leadership styles that are redolent of heroism. They see the linkages between such leaders and death, destruction and tyranny. Yet the majority of us – men and women – do not let go of what-ever hopes and desires are locked up in such leaders. This is the split, and it would be *hubris* for anyone to claim to have got over it. The *idea* of the hero will not go away. Even when a leader decides to become a democratic sort of person, and walk down Constitutional Avenue or play head-tennis with a soccer star, as did Jimmy Carter or Tony Blair, the very delib-erateness of such anti-heroic, democratic, man-of-the-people stances, reveals that they trade off the heroic thing. No anti-hero without a hero in mind.

Psychotherapy has something to say about why it is so hard to let go emotionally of the idea of leader-as-hero, even while knowing intellectually and cognitively that it is no use at all to have heroic leaders. Broadly speaking, the split exists for reasons to do with identification. Many people feel deeply enhanced by the kinds of fantasies that take place in identifi-cation with a heroic leader. Erase the heroic projection and you spoil the pleasures of identification. We come to feel in some way denuded or deprived. So, although we know that heroic leaders are passé, dangerous and destructive, that they leave out whole sections of the community (who are then excluded from power, and not part of the body politic), it is proving extremely difficult to get beyond heroic models.

One aim in raising the idea of good-enough leadership is to see whether there are non-heroic images of leadership that can inspire people emotionally and psychologically in the way that heroic models do. Or, to put it in the language of political process and experience, to see whether we can infuse into networked, collaborative, bottom-up organizational models the same kinds of energic charge that we see all too clearly at work in top-down, heroically led, hierarchical organizations such as the modern state. To use the vernacular, can one make co-operation, participation and networking sexy and beloved, just as the dominant-submissive, heroism-infected, leader-led relationship is?

Up until now, we have discussed failed leaders and the failure of the idea of heroic leadership in our time. What about making fuller use of the proposition that failure is at the heart of good-enoughness? *A good-enough leader has to be an artist in failure.* Most leaders have enormous difficulty coming to terms with the inevitability of failure. People have often noted how hard it is for politicians even to say that they have changed their minds about something, as though that in itself were an admission of failure. As Mrs Thatcher put it, 'the lady's not for turning'. It is also extremely interesting to see how hard it is for leaders to accept that what they are proposing may well not work out or succeed as planned. They find it difficult to understand that failure comes with the political territory, that, in fact, leadership requires proficiency in the art of failure.

When Ulrich Beck, the German sociologist, talks about 'risk societies', he guides us in the general direction of an acceptance of impotence and failure.[4] In the late-modern age, governments and leaders often cannot deal with the problems they are faced with because they do not know in advance what those problems are going to be. In Britain, BSE, 'mad cow disease', was a classic example of a risk that almost nobody in authority had anticipated. Similar unpredictable problems, such as the problem of genetically modified foods, are going to arise with increasing frequency as societies become ever more complex and fragmented. Many risks are simply beyond the comprehension and the capacity of governments to cope with.

The 'uncertainty principle' that we know about from physics also operates in politics. The more prepared for one crisis, the less prepared for another. Leadership becomes less and less a question of succeeding at coping with the challenges and the risks that a modern society faces and more and more a question of ameliorating the inevitable failure to deal with those risks and challenges. So a leader who is artful, a leader who is competent, a good-enough leader, is not a leader who solves things. She or he is a leader who well manages their own failure to solve the problems that confront the community. A 'can't do politician'.

A further psychological reason that we have to accept the inevitability of failure has to do with the unconscious itself. The human psyche is the source of much in the world that is creative, benevolent, artistic, spiritual, lovely. It is also the source of much that is horrible, shitty, aggressive, life-destroying and conducive to planetary destruction. This bothness of the human psyche – maybe we could call it not only the good-enough but also the 'bad-enough' psyche – is something with which, politically and psychologically, we have an enormous problem. It has never been easy to accept that there are limits on what can be done in the social realm given the nasty, shadow side of being human. If leadership is the art of failure, good-enough leaders may have to acknowledge that not only will we fail to do what we want to do because problems are difficult to solve but because, as humans, we are flawed problem solvers, always and already failures at getting things done.

This is an opportunity to add a somewhat old-fashioned and earthy political comment to these psychological observations. People of goodwill, good heart and progressive opinions cannot simply prevail as they wish to because, in any society, there are elements, structures and institutions that do not wish them to prevail. Politics is not a level playing field and, while the human psyche may have contributed to this state of affairs, it is not a purely psychological problem. In many Western societies, inequalities and discrepancies have been getting worse and worse. Vested interests, structural imbalances and economic theories mean that, even if Labour or Democratic leaders truly wanted to distribute wealth and work towards social justice, there are forces that will always seriously limit their goals.

GOOD-ENOUGH LEADERS

What follows is a sketch of three kinds of good-enough leaders, each of whom is ultimately a failure, or incomplete as a leader, while still providing something vitally important to the citizenry. The idea is not to relate these images in any precise way to specific leaders or politicians because these are not people, they are imaginary creations. Although it is not hard to think of a leader who corresponds to one or more of these images, that would be a fortuitous accident and not central to the main point.

First, the *erotic leader*. Despite what many readers may at first think, an erotic leader is not one who hops in and out of bed. In many countries, public obsession with the sex lives of leaders suggests that there is something about the actual, physical, corporeal eroticism of leadership that is worth exploring further. The concern of the media with the sexuality of leading figures in society generally, not just political leaders, suggests that, as in many similar instances, mass consciousness has discovered something interesting about a complicated problem.

Erotic leaders use their sexuality to convey to citizens that they (the citizens) are exciting, creative and autonomous people who can work co-operatively together. Receiving ordinary admiration and warmth are extremely potent parts of psychological evolution and establishing self-esteem. Whether leaders do or do not communicate to people in an almost physically warm way that they admire them is an interesting and neglected aspect of the political process. Maybe leaders, so to speak, lend their own sense of being admired to the people – or maybe they simply return it.

The model for this notion is the work done on parenting, focusing on 'erotic playback'.[5] As noted in the preceding chapters, this is the way the parent communicates to children of both sexes that they are admirable, physically desirable and erotically viable creatures. (I repeat: I am referring only to incest fantasy here, not to the destructive physical enactment of such fantasy.) Western societies seem to me to mirror Western families in that the subtle damage and deprivation caused by erotic *deficit* is far less spoken of than that of erotic *excess*. Actual physical incest takes place appallingly often, and it is important to recognize that and mobilize against it. But something equally central and much more benevolent in sexuality (especially male sexuality) is being overlooked. Moreover, the consequences of an absence of such positive sexuality are also overlooked.

The reference to the erotic includes sex, but has to do with more than sex. It involves harmony, relatedness, purpose, significance and meaning: Eros. As we know from psychoanalysis and Jungian psychology, sexuality is involved or implicated in all these things in some way and at some level. That means, of course, that ambivalence, anxiety, jealousy, rivalry and the sense that something is lacking – the rudiments of failure – will also be present in the picture.

How does the erotic leader function? The erotic leader can be a good-enough leader of whatever sex. I will paint the picture according to the actual sex of the leader and the actual sex of the citizen, though bearing in mind that we probably still know more about men as erotic leaders than we do about women. These relational paradigms between leaders and citizens operate on both the conscious and unconscious levels.

The erotic leader not only makes citizens feel good and beautiful at a very deep, almost bodily level, but also brings out and reflects back the healthy self-love and self-admiration that exists in everyone. This admiration contributes to their feeling honoured, at first for a moment and then lastingly, in their internal diversity. Because sexual identity is not a unified, fixed, static, eternal, universal thing, erotic playback as communicated to the citizens by the erotic leader encourages citizens to think of themselves in a diversified way, to come alive and hold together in the mind all aspects of the self: public and private, active and passive, political and psychological. Because sex carries such a diversified charge, sexual recognition by an erotic leader can lead to – encourage – citizens' recognition of themselves as a diversified being.

Above all, there is something about the way in which sexual dynamics switch between domination and submission on the part of the individual involved that make them particularly relevant for a discussion of this particular kind of leader – the erotic leader. Switching between psychological domination and submission is something quite missing in Western polities no matter what lip-service is paid to the supremacy of the ballot box. Where are the submissive leaders? Where are the dominant citizenries? In our inner lives, and in our relationships, we surely know about this switching. The erotic leader can create a micro-environment in which the citizen is allowed to switch between submission and domination in relation to the leader – a state of affairs reminiscent of Jean Genet's play *The Balcony*, in which there is a special kind of brothel: the police chief dresses up as a criminal and the bishop can wear the garments of a prostitute.

When the erotic leader is a male, he makes a female citizen feel other than maternal. Of course mothers are sexy. But there is something about the creative force of female sexuality that can be distinguished from maternal creativity. The male erotic leader works with the female citizen to enable her to go beyond the traditional and socially restrictive virtues of relation and care.

*When the erotic leader is male and the citizen is male, homoso-
ciality arises between them* – fraternity in action. We saw this
in operation in gay communities which experimented with
new political forms in order to come to grips with the issues
presented by HIV/AIDS. There is something politically challenging about the homosociality that a male erotic leader
and a male citizen can develop between them.

*When the erotic leader is female, and the citizen is male, she
offers that male citizen a chance to merge with her* as a symbol
of the earth, against the prevailing psychotherapy orthodoxy
which says that symbiosis and merger with the feminine or
the mother is a very bad thing for a man. What we could call
ecomasculinism (men who care passionately for the environment) needs a political climate in which female erotic leaders
create circumstances that enable male citizens to merge with
them (the female leaders taking on for a moment the traditional, earthy role of women).

*When the erotic leader is female and the citizen is female, the
citizen is offered a very special and different approach to power,
rivalry and competition.* Such a couple are not going to be
stuck in some sort of false sisterhood. They are going to be
politically rivalrous and competitive with each other. But,
given that it will be an all-female political dynamic, it will be
an unusual kind of rivalry, less dominated by male values,
and, in its femaleness, not necessarily structured by penis,
phallus or rivalry for possession of them. (For a fuller
account of female–female rivalry, see Chapter 7.)

To summarize: when the erotic leader is male, he helps
females to feel like something besides mothers and helps

males to participate in homosocial action. When the erotic leader is female, she offers males a chance to merge creatively with her and offers females an approach to power, rivalry and competition other than the one that men have laid out.

There are dimensions to these ideas that go beyond individual functioning. Like human sexuality, human society is exceedingly diverse. The suggestion is that there are links between a full flowering of diverse, pluralistic human sexuality and a full flowering of diverse, pluralistic human culture. These more collective potentials, too, may be activated by the erotic leader. The sense of admiration and respect for the full range of sexual diversity can cross over into the processes that enable societies to sustain cultural diversity – for example, ethnic or class diversity. When sexual desire is in operation, fixed psychological identities and rules cease to play the part that they are supposed to. Then we are more prepared for the challenge of living in an increasingly diversified culture in which fixed social identities and rules are also undermined.

Of course, I am trying to synthesize a massive body of work on the relations between gender and sexuality on the one hand and ethnicity and 'raciality' on the other.[6] Succinctly put, between colonizer and colonized there has always been a kind of masculine–feminine divide. The British were the 'masculine' conquerors to the 'feminine' conquered of the Indians of the sub-continent, or to the Irish. Erotic playback from a good-enough erotic leader destabilizes who is masculine and who is feminine. It destabilizes 'colonial' relations within particular cultures like Britain or the United States. The erotic leader not only makes the citizen feel good and admired; there is also a positive communication about collective diversity.

Erotic leaders are most definitely not always men, though Nelson Mandela may exemplify erotic leadership. Towards the end of her life, Princess Diana emerged as a kind of erotic leader on the psychological level being explored here. She was not only the combination of mother and sexual icon which many commentators noted but also an image of *maternal sexuality*, where the two are already joined. The topic of maternal sexuality is, of course, highly emotive and taboo. The French psychoanalyst Jean Laplanche posits that 'what inspires psychological growth is the seductiveness of the (m)other'.[7] By the action of her sexuality and via erotic playback, she seduces the growth potential out of the child, who longs to join with her in a relationship and so must 'move' and grow in order to do so. For Laplanche, this primary seductiveness accounts for the origins of the psyche itself, which is, so to speak, drawn out of the individual by something sexual.

Princess Diana certainly drew out people's psyches, which why it is reasonable to see her not simply as 'mother plus sex', but as an image of maternal sexuality itself. When this topic is discussed, the 'seductive mother' is often seen as a bad one in the professional literature. Yet without her seduction of and erotic playback to the child there would be no psychic activity or growth. If this overall analysis is in any way pertinent, then Princess Diana's life and death are symbolic examples of the primary seduction of maternal sexuality and erotic playback, and it was we, the public, who were (healthily) seduced and led. The public mood at the time of her death contained all the energy you would expect to see when it is drawn out by this kind of erotic playback, which is carried by the maternal body. Diana's maternal sexuality and her qualities of erotic leadership were experienced as quite literally drawing the potential out of people.

I will end this sketch of the erotic leader by reiterating that leadership played in a good-enough key inevitably involves failure. (It could even be argued that a too successful erotic leader will inaugurate a special and spectacular order of failure.) Erotic leaders will fail because there are real difficulties for the citizen in taking this type of leader inside her or himself so as to relate 'erotically' to other people in society. Many citizens will fail to care for each other in ways that are congruent with the messages they receive from an erotic leader. So the whole business of erotic leadership will not completely work as hoped. For example, the giving of erotic playback may stay very much the sole property of a narcissistic leader. Moreover, you cannot just clobber people into feeling better about themselves. In our world, and maybe in all possible worlds, we have to face that many people do not and will never feel good about themselves. Consider how many of Roget's categories for synonyms of 'failure' have a personal flavour: impotence, bungling, loser, loss, object of scorn. Failure always takes us back to something personal.

The second image of the good-enough leader is *Trickster-as-leader*. Once again, we need to begin with a clarification. Tricksters in politics are not necessarily identical with the practice of dirty tricks in politics. I am certainly not going to say we need more dirty tricks, sleaze, backhanders or undeclared interests. Tricksters are legendary or mythic figures, found in many cultures, who tend to defy the laws of reality – laws of time, space and place. For the Greeks, the arch-Trickster was Hermes, the messenger of the gods, the deity of change, known for his tendency to play jokes, to lie, to steal, to cheat, to deny physical and social reality, and to engage in grandiose fantasy. When Hermes steals Apollo's cattle, he drives them backwards to his home stable in order to fool the god of order's pursuing posse. When Apollo tries to capture him, the ropes which are supposed to bind Hermes snake off in all directions. When Apollo and Hermes resolve their differences by an exchange of gifts, the links between criminality and creativity are established and celebrated.

In the carnivals of the Middle Ages, an unsuitable person, such as a child or the village idiot, would be dressed up as the bishop. In fairy tales, we find figures like Tom Thumb taking an anti-heroic role. Parapsychology is full of Tricksterish poltergeists who challenge the boundaries of what we take for reality. Animals often represent the Trickster in politics (Machiavelli's famous fox is a good example). Most Tricksters, from Coyote in North America to Anansi or Eshu in West Africa, follow this pattern, subverting the social hierarchy, undermining the prevailing organization of power and even the perceived structure of reality itself. For example, Anansi manages to trick the wealthy Akwasi so that Akwasi actually ends up ordering Anansi to make love to his wife Aso.

Anthropologists have suggested that the cultural function of Tricksters is to destabilize the social order. Tricksters are in-house revolutionaries. Of course, the Trickster's discourse is not usually as articulate as this makes it seem. After all, the Trickster is, according to Jung, a symbol of the unconscious itself. When politics becomes little more than dirty tricks and backroom deals, we are seeing only a tiny and distorted part of the Trickster theme in action, and much else about the Trickster is simply overlooked if we permit our moralizing zeal to get the better of us. Tricksters enhance our notion of leadership by virtue of their visionary, rule-breaking capacity. They are revolutionary simply because they are not rooted in codified reality.

Understandably, some readers may have a mixed reaction to the idea of assigning a political value to what is essentially the immature personality. We are indeed talking about the political yield that stems from people who have not grown up and the potential political value of grandiose fantasy. But this is meant to be a politics of play, of unbridled creativity, of Romantic and Bohemian sensibilities. Tricksters are not dictators; they have not got the attention span. We can claim Tricksters for the political because what they do is dispute what we call realism on the one hand and idealism on the other. They simply do not know that there is supposed to be a difference! For them, there is *only* 'the vision thing'.

Yet Tricksters introduce us to more than a laudable and much needed visionary politics. Trickster politics involves bringing a dreamy and playful out-of-touch-with-reality viewpoint into politics. This perspective is something that contemporary Western politics also needs, and something that requires Trickster leadership to bring about. We are talking about ingenuity, improvisation, flexibility, rule-breaking, seeing things differently, doing things differently, not being hidebound, being open to change, being open to failure. This concerns the kind of skills that we sometimes see in the parallel (or 'black') economy that exists alongside the official economic system in Third World countries. If the official statistics told the true story about economic activity in some countries, everyone would have died long ago. But unlicensed unofficial trade is surviving, whether in the shanty towns of Latin America or the villages of Somalia (not to mention North London). Spontaneously formed economic and social organizations are full of Tricksterism and need Trickster energies to get going.

Western politics places great stress on the formal constitutional structures and decision-making processes. In its devotion to formality, mainstream politics has often lost the ability to access the vital and innovatory dimensions that Tricksters bring into play. So, while Trickster leaders, if we were to categorize them, certainly have the potential to carry out all sorts of ugly, dirty tricks, they also have the potential to be extremely intuitive, ingenious, improvisatory and creative in the practice of politics.

Trickster leaders will fail, just as the erotic leader will fail. They will fail because anybody who tries to live *exclusively* as a Trickster will simply and quite correctly not be trusted, and will be unlikely to achieve high office. Nevertheless, most of us have seen Trickster leaders in action: somebody in an organization (often a person low down in the hierarchy) has a crazy idea and everyone thinks yet again that this person is a real liability. Then, suddenly, you find that the off-the-wall thing they said a few weeks ago has turned out to be surprisingly worthy of trust.

Never forget that it is the solid folk, well placed in the hierarchy, nary a Trickster among them, the ones who follow orders and know the ropes, who often do the cruel and nasty thing in organizations, playing the power games, performing the backstabbings, carrying out the exclusions and executions. It is the mature, rounded, realistic people who sometimes hold the whole thing back, and deal out the nasty stuff. But they are not really mature if they have no vision. It is the apparently harmless visionaries, leaders who may not know too well who they are as people or even that they are actually leaders, who, every now and again, get results. Several people have commented to me that Gandhi and even Jesus come to mind as Trickster leaders.

We can see signs that the way the psyche is evolving in Western societies tends to foster the emergence of more female Trickster leaders. Sometimes the female Trickster enters the political arena by overdoing, in a transgressive manner, what is prescribed for women. For example, the Mothers of the Plaza de Mayo helped to topple the Argentine Junta by assembling, dressed in full maternal mourning dress, in the main square of Buenos Aires. They wore the embroidered scarves of bereavement, but stitched on each scarf was the name and date of disappearance of their child or children. The regulations about exchanging such information were evaded. The Mothers made good use of the sacred feeling that Argentines, even torturers, have towards mothers.

Another area where we can see today's female Tricksters in leadership roles is in the environmental movement. The equation of women and nature or earth can be (but is not necessarily) one of the most oppressive equations for women when culture and power are then left for men. But when the equation of woman equals earth is exaggerated and parodied, as in some forms of ecofeminism, a new kind of energy becomes available for politics. An illustration of this is in Margaret Atwood's novel *Surfacing* where the female narrator melts into the earth, becoming a hybrid human, animal, ghost – and gains power over her 'American' persecutors in the process.

The list of contemporary female Tricksters is almost endless. I think of the crop of female private investigators like V. I. Warshawski or sexually open film stars like Sharon Stone with her one-liner that 'having a vagina and a point of view is a deadly combination'. Maybe some will say that the struggle for autonomy that characterizes the life of any and every woman in Western (or, indeed, non-Western) societies makes her a female Trickster already. Perhaps. But the main point is that the blatant political flavour of the female Trickster highlights the argument with which we began: that political cultures need Tricksters as leaders and this is a far more complicated matter than the question of truth or falsehood, honesty or dishonesty, trustworthiness or untrustworthiness, in political conduct would suggest.

I am not so naive as simply to say that we need carnival politics and all will be well. But the notion that politics can have a carnivalesque element to it has been around for a long time. In our political lifetime we have seen examples of carnival politics in the Yippies of 1968, the Situationists, and the whole way in the 1970s and 1980s in which the anti-nuclear protestors took a symbolic, gestural, Tricksterish path. In Britain, protesters knitted a gigantic scarf to 'warm' a US airforce nuclear base. This kind of Tricksterish, playful behaviour is in marked contrast to the merely dishonest, as well as to the hypocritically solemn behaviour of so many mainstream politicians.

The third example of good-enough leadership is *sibling leadership*, and I prepared the ground for this idea in Chapters 4 and 5. This is a psychological way to deconstruct the notion of leadership altogether. What follows is a take on decentralized, non-hierarchical, networked, bottom-up, highly democratic ways of organizing things. The question of leadership should not be ignored for many of these experimental forms of social organization have foundered because they dared not address the problem of leadership.

Let me ask my readers to review everything that I have already mentioned in this book concerning the sibling relationship, especially the brother–sister relationship. The usual sibling themes of friendship, enmity, attraction, repulsion, alliance, rivalry, rebellion, seeking the favours of the more powerful – aren't these markedly political themes? And, stemming from the Bible perhaps, Cain and Abel, Isaac and Ishmael, Jacob and Esau – don't siblings usually get a bad press? Conversely, Antigone's story, or that of Hansel and Gretel, alert us to the positive, political and caring role that this relationship can play when tyranny is afoot.

In our gender-conscious times, many citizens want to play whatever part they choose in the political process firmly within their own sex. This has been especially true for women but is becoming increasingly the case for men as well: 'I am not just a citizen, I'm a male (or female) citizen.' But if a gender-conscious citizen does not want to engage in a 1960s or early 1970s gender separatist style of politics, but instead wants to work in alliance with members of the other sex who have similar values and aims, what are they to do? We know that male and female agendas are different, so how can one do politics as a man but in alliance with women? Many people experience this as a problem. They definitely do not want to be bland, sexless citizens, without an acknowledgement of differences, especially different political goals for the two sexes. But at the same time they do not want only to work politically with or support members of their own sex. They tend to shelve the problem and get on with things as best they can.

In part, this happens because, in the West, we lack images and models to foster our doing politics as women or men but in some kind of explicit and consciously-entered-into temporary deal or alliance with the other sex. This book is an attempt to provide such images and models. The aim is for people to function openly as sexed citizens but not as separatist sexed citizens. Conventional political discourse does not admit this kind of differentiation. Romantic love does not really supply useful imagery or a model on which to build a political organization, largely because such love is so incredibly absorbing of the time and energy of the people involved. Marriage as an image really does not work here either, because marriage, we know, has its own particular and peculiar politics – its own oppressions, its own imbalances, its own property laws.

So I have turned to siblings as an image of an alliance between female and male citizens (though without forgetting same-sex sibling relationships, the politics of which, unsurprisingly, has been much better theorized thanks to feminism and lesbian and gay political theorists). Central to the idea of siblings as leaders is, as we have seen, a politicization or re-politicization of the horizontal dimension of being a sibling. Sexed citizens can access the radicality and autonomy that informs the pre-adolescent children's struggle with their parents. It is a mistake to see rebellion against authority as solely located in or predefined by adolescence. While this might be true for individuals, the opposite happens in connection with the sibling relationship. In their ineluctable resistance to parental and societal authority, siblings speak for a decentralized style of leadership that eschews the erection of authority figures (thereby building in its eventual failure, as we shall see).

The hope is that sibling leadership would imply networking and non-hierarchical ways of communicating and decision-making without its becoming bland or homogenizing into a simulacrum of management consultancy. The existence of sibling leaders could never totally replace other kinds of leaders. But, by thinking of modern leadership in terms derived from sibling models, we undercut the notion of heroic leadership itself without denying the phenomenon. As suggested earlier, the rapid and easy exchange of information through the Internet might also be seen as a re-emergence of sibling politics on the cultural level. Pre-adolescent siblings do not keep secrets from each other; they co-educate each other. That is what gets lost in adolescence.

If we regard sibling leadership as a mode of leadership, we enter the politics of ambivalence that was introduced earlier. We are once more talking the language of temporary political alliance or coalition between citizens of both sexes. Progressive politics has trouble embracing the ethos of temporary deal-making that capitalists and patriarchs are very comfortable with because politically progressive types have such high ideals. They want to agree completely with the people they are doing their politics with. Many political activists spend so much time and energy on the political equivalents of wanting to be in love, wanting to be married to each other, without realizing that these old stories about relationships in action are really quite conservative.

Sibling leaders will also fail. This is because, unfortunately, the siblings, full of radical imagination, all too soon become the parents, full of a new and pressing desire to keep the status quo and even to turn the clock back, retaining power as they go. Sibling leadership, although good-enough in all the ways the term has been used, fails because the siblings grow up and lose their radical edge. Nevertheless, leadership failure, like parental failure on the personal level, spurs on the growth of autonomy and activism. Leadership failure leaves political spaces within which citizens can *act*.

DRAWING TOGETHER

What I have tried to do is to position some ideas about good-enough leadership against a background of a transformative politics. Good-enough leaders are quite powerful from an energic point of view, but relatively powerless from the point of view of conventional political power and influence. Good-enoughness, which is a concept that all therapists and counsellors are familiar with, has also got out into the culture, because, when steering a middle course between idealization and denigration or dependence and autonomy, it speaks to people's experience. Good-enoughness seems particularly relevant to the problem of leadership, for good-enoughness involves letting people down to a degree that they can learn to manage. In turn, certain kinds of failures will take place. If we think about leadership in terms of the management of such failure, the results are worthwhile. The three particular images that I have wanted to share with readers are of particular interest to me; others will find other images via which to address the perennial problem of leadership.

CHAPTER SEVEN

The good-enough father of whatever sex

L'être dont l'être est de n'être pas
(The being whose essence is in not having an essence)

Simone de Beauvoir

THE FATHER IN CONTEMPORARY POLITICS

In Britain and the United States, the pivotal place of lone-parent families in public debates about families and family policies remains a feature of the political scene. In 1995, the then Conservative government announced plans to cut the benefits payable to lone-parent families and the early days of the 1997 Labour government were also marked by an attempt to cut such payments. The American story has been very similar.

Not surprisingly, then, when there are meetings about lone-parent family issues, they often take place in a politicized and tense atmosphere, with media interest and demonstrations. In such a situation, it is not too farfetched to say that developmental psychology and psychotherapeutic perspectives on family process move implicitly and secretly to the heart of political life. Hence the presence of a chapter on 'the father' in a book on politics.

The chapter is both a psychological response to the challenge of fatherhood and a critique of social policies based on received wisdoms about the father. It tries to break up the monolith called father by introducing two figures whom I call the 'good-enough father' and the 'father of whatever sex'.

The idea is to show that there is both more and less to fathers than the continuing political and moral panic about lone parenthood suggests. If we listen to the psychological subtext of the passionate debate about the social and political consequences of lone parenthood being conducted in most of the West, it becomes clear that we are witnessing a damaging and misleading idealization of fathers and the roles men play in families. It is folly to base policy on this idealization. But the fact that such idealization exists gives political debate in the 1990s about lone parenthood a marked psychological dimension. The politics revolve around psychological theory and the psychology has become part of political debate.

What drives the continuing stigmatization of women who bring up children alone in many Western countries is our world's total failure to come to terms with the imminent collapse of some of the things that used to support male dominance in society – a collective failure that, as we have seen in previous chapters, has left many men unsure of their personal roles. Generally speaking, men still have the power, but they lack a fixed identity. As the British suicide figures for the 1990s show, this unsettles them so much that they find living with it difficult or impossible. Male suicide almost doubled; female suicide declined by about the same amount. It cannot simply be unemployment, for there have been recessions before.

It often seems that the only thing that governments, various sections of the media, certain academics and many therapists are able to do is to yearn for the return of the father as a source of stability, discipline and order in the family and, by some kind of magic, in society as well. This yearning persists in spite of what we now know about the so-called 'traditional' family; it was a very short-lived phenomenon (if it ever existed at all). As several recent historical studies have shown, the family has always mutated in a duet with economic and industrial organization.[1] That is why it is so important not to fall for the temptations of underclass theory and pillory today's lone parents and their families – never mind the scarcely hidden racism in that tendency. It is pointless to yearn for yesterday's ideal family. That family, source of much misery, was a staging post on a long journey. In fact, in Britain today, only a minority of families (about 23 per cent) consist of the conventional mixture of a male breadwinner, a female homemaker and two children. As Helen Wilkinson put it, as far as families are concerned, 'diversity is king'.[2]

In the mode of yearning to which so many segments of society seem addicted, the father is presented as a sort of public school 'fagmaster', the older boy who is assigned younger boys as servants and in return helps to form their characters. A first leader in *The Times* in 1993 showed this up very well by bemoaning the absence of fathers as a 'moral presence' in the family. The trouble is that, when faced with thinking like this, there is a vacuum where new ideas should exist.

Even in progressive circles there is a denial of the possibility of other styles and models of fathering. Perhaps we can come up with a model here, based on views and values that will neither implicitly condemn lone-parent, fatherless families nor leave them in the lurch. Such a model of fatherhood would stress the father's active, direct emotional involvement with his children from the earliest age. It would support an egalitarian, co-operative, non-hierarchical family, rather than pointlessly seeking to restore father and his authority as the (flawed) source of rules and regulations – whereby, presumably, he would also be reinstated as the source of sexual and physical abuse of women and children.

While not denying that many clients from lone-parent family backgrounds have psychological problems, twenty-five years of clinical research into lone-parent families leads me to dispute that there are *inevitable* damaging psychological effects of living in a lone-parent family. Damage would be still less inevitable were lone-parent families to be given adequate resources, approval and support from the community. When we talk about resources, we should perhaps think of more than money, housing and so forth – although these are clearly important. We should also think of what it does to the evolving personality of a child in a lone-parent family to know that the set-up at home is attacked in the real, adult world as inferior, bad, mad and in need of government control. My own children certainly picked up quite specific social and political values and assumptions about family life from television before they were 5 years old.

PLAYING THE FATHER ROLE

There are two separate questions involved in the psycho-cultural debate over fatherhood. The first has to do with the consequences (or lack of them) of lone parenthood for child development. For convenience, we could call this *the lone-mother question*. The second has to do with the question of what fathering *is* these days. We could call this *the crisis-in-fatherhood question*. It is important to recognize that these two apparently different questions lead us in a surprisingly similar direction. Addressing one question helps us to engage with the other. Both questions stimulate thinking about what fathers do, or can do, that is life-affirming and related to others, beyond being a 'moral presence'.

We can begin to create and assemble a psychological information pool, or resource, for women bringing up children on their own or women bringing up children together with other women. When the father is revisioned as being 'unpatriarchal', such women can also be revisioned, not only as mothers but also as 'fathers of whatever sex'. Immediately, we undermine everything that our society assigns or wishes to assign to men. Anatomy ceases to determine parental destiny and the lone-mother question is completely reframed.

The questions we need to ask of women are: can you do the things that male fathers do? Do you *want* to do them? We invite women to assert their capacities to be fathers of whatever sex, which would often make them good-enough fathers, rather than setting them up to fail as phoney ideal fathers. Men fail to be ideal fathers, too. Women may well choose not to perform every item on any list of fatherly functions, nor will they necessarily perform these functions in *precisely* the same way that men might. But would that matter? Some might say it would be a pretty good thing. Difference does not always mean deficit. The issue is not that mothering and fathering are identical – though there will be disagreement about the differences – but whether or not a woman can do much of what fathers do (and a man much of what mothers do).

Gathering information about fathering today could enable women to decide how many of its functions they could perform themselves. That is why the usual formulation has been twisted so as to call women who raise children alone good-enough fathers. Many women who raise children alone, or together with other women, are certainly already doing a lot of being a good-enough father of whatever sex without naming it as such. This group of women represents an incalculably valuable resource. What they do as parents could herald a whole new approach to parenting that plugs into the fluidity in gender roles that has evolved since the Second World War which is not going to be wished and/or legislated away by governments.

To those who have a negative reaction to the idea that women can be good-enough fathers and play the father's role, let us say: men, too, only *play* the father's role. Fathering does not come 'naturally' to men, along with penises and stubble – it has to be learned, and every new father discovers that society has rules about how to do it; there is a masquerade of manliness, a male masquerade, to adapt Joan Rivière's term.[3] Women who father as good-enough fathers of whatever sex may teach things to men who father. I remember my daughter setting up a game with me by saying, 'You be the daddy, Daddy' – and then, at some point in our family play, announcing, 'Now I'll be the daddy, Daddy'.

This is the bottom-line lived experience behind the academic work on power and on the cultural construction of gender and gender roles.[4] Men already play the role of father, just as women may come to play the role. And they play it differently at different times and in different places; parenting is inherently multicultural. It is surely significant how much we all use the word 'role' in relation to being a parent. So, for the sake of completeness, let us recall that women who look after very small children are *playing* at being mothers, playing the role of mother. Motherhood, too, is not as 'natural' as some people continue delusively to think it is. Maternity and paternity have evolving histories.

What of the second question, the question of the crisis in fatherhood, what fatherhood is and means for men? We certainly need to make the role of the male parent more interesting and meaningful for younger men who have started to reject a dictatorial, Jurassic style of fathering – even if their female partners would accept such behaviour, which, these days, is unlikely. Women's increasing refusal to accept male dominance, coupled with men's beginning search for inspiring ideas about manhood and fatherhood, are crucial social and psychological changes on which the debate about fathers should be focusing. 'Men' have become a category, one of many, rather than some sort of privileged vantage point. But, as noted earlier, this huge change in Western consciousness does not mean that men and women now have identical agendas. Men will not give up their power that easily, and there is a lot of making up to be done. But writing as a man, a father, a therapist, I have come to see that it is not the actual maleness of the person from whom the child obtains fathering that is important. What matters is whether or not the relationship between the father of whatever sex and her or his children is good enough.

This chapter works on two levels: as a resource for women who raise children alone, and as an agenda for contemporary men who want to be fathers in a new way that is psychologically realistic. To underscore the two levels and to explain the terms and words used, let me pose a series of questions. When a man takes care of a very small baby, what should we call what he does? *Fathering*, part of an enhanced and expanded definition of father? *Mothering*, because looking after the newborn is what mothers traditionally do? Or plain parenting? Similarly, if a woman lays down the law in a family, is she *mothering*, part of an enhanced and expanded definition of a mother? Or is she *fathering*, because laying down the law is what fathers traditionally do? Or plain parenting?

If we opt for straightforward answers or desex the words for parents, we deny any differences between mothers and fathers. The questions show that our language for parenting has collapsed; that is why some want so desperately to speak a language they need to believe once existed. But the breakdown is not a disaster. It is an opportunity, and ushers in a new kind of transformative politics, fuelled by what people actually experience in their emotional and personal lives.

THE POLITICS OF PATERNAL WARMTH

In Chapters 4 and 5, I argued that, in all the justified concern about child sexual abuse, we have perhaps forgotten to say enough about the positive aspects of a father's physical warmth. Many conventional families have lacked this kind of experience, a lack that can generate its own particularly pernicious brand of psychic pain. Any woman bringing up children alone or together with another woman is bound to give some thought to what it means that there is no father present. Here, she will think about the positive outcomes of providing fatherly warmth. She will want to decide whether or not to attempt to become the father of whatever sex, whether or not to try to provide similar experiences leading to similar outcomes, and how to do this.

Fatherly warmth leads to a recognition of daughters as people in their own right, not simply as little mothers, not only as creatures tied into the image and role of mother. As we saw, this has sociopolitical implications. Many feminist writers have shown convincingly that the 'reproduction of mothering' is terribly limiting for women. It ties them into the role of the one who looks after others, who responds and reacts to their needs, who puts her own needs last and who dares not risk disfavour and disapproval by expressing her assertiveness and demands. Fatherly recognition of the daughter as other than a mother can enable women to break out of the cycle of the reproduction of motherhood. Those other pathways that I mentioned earlier then emerge: the spiritual path, the work path, the path that integrates her assertive side, the path of sexual expression (not necessarily heterosexual), maybe the path of celibacy. It is crucial that there be pathways that are not man-oriented and that involve movement away from the father – for example, the path of solidarity and community with other women.

Women bringing up children alone can send similar messages to their daughters. They can understand and recognize their daughters' evolving sexual potential – and everyone has a sexual potential from birth – as taking those daughters away from a mix-up or overlap with the mother. The stress on the sexual daughter is deliberate here; mothers, too, can be sexual. A recognition of a daughter's evolving sexuality by either a female or a male parent plays a part in turning that daughter away from a path in life that is completely circumscribed by the maternal role. To function as the father of whatever sex may mean a woman who parents alone will actually seek out and accentuate the competition that goes on in families between parents and children of the same sex. The mother can communicate to her daughter that the daughter is a potential rival (in many diverse respects, not just Oedipal rivalry over a father). She can go on to communicate that this is not a bad thing and, if she does, she will make possible the kind of differentiation from the mother that a male father's recognition provides.

Paternal warmth challenges our cultural habit of splitting perceptions of the male body into something horribly abusive and violent (which it can be) or something meekly pretty, hairless and nice (which it usually is not). Nevertheless, male bodies have potential to do good as well as harm, and discussion about *both* possibilities will take us far beyond the idealized images of advertising.

Communicating positive physical warmth is pleasant and moving for both participants. The father as well as the daughter receives something out of this 'erotic playback'. Once the initial 'woman equals mother' equation is broken up, the outcome for a girl is unpredictable. She may want and need to grow away from as well as towards her father, away from the world of men in general as well as towards it, to seek out, work with, fall in love with and raise children with other women.

Fathers do not simply liberate or permit daughters to take up different psychosocial roles from that of maternity, but foster a *plurality* of psychosocial roles, meaning the ways in which they do or do not shake down for women into a workable blend of oneness and manyness. This is a key social issue for women – how to be more than one person while at the same time still managing to stay psychologically whole? The many mainstream books about superwoman and her balancing act with her time indicate that these ideas about the father–daughter connection are not just of professional psychological interest.

What about the father's physical warmth and erotic playback in relation to the son? For sons, a good-enough physical connection to the father helps lead to the growth of homosociality. The political implications of this are immense. Intimate father–son relating, prompted by positive physical warmth that is frankly expressed between them, could inspire the new forms of social and political organization that Western societies urgently need just now – emphasizing co-operation and non-hierarchical organization as modes of masculinity that are just as valid as the pecking order and the rat race. They are also modes of being that women will find more congenial than aping all the worst features of the male drive for success.

In these new forms of social organization, men learn from other men just as they love them. As far as fathering is concerned, we saw in Chapter 5 that the most difficult hurdle to overcome is the fear that ordinary, devoted, good-enough fathers will somehow be effeminate, the code for 'homosexual'. Our culture has employed a fear and loathing of homosexuality as a weapon to keep men tied into the role of provider in the family, the ones who must therefore remain emotionally distant. The pay-off for men has been access to economic and political power. The cost has been the loss of the opportunity for intimacy and the expression of paternal warmth.

This is territory where the female father of whatever sex comes into *her* own and can function as a resource for male fathers. Women tend to know more about community and non-hierarchical organization from the inside. Women who parent alone will probably already be considering how to make co-operation more attractive to their sons, rather than having them regard it as bland or, worse, non-manly. They may use what power they have to reinforce and support an *absence* of hierarchy and unbendable rules, asking, even challenging their sons to use their imaginations as much as their biceps. And many sons will respond to the challenge. They know at some level that being an old-style, oppositional man, testing the limits of authority, is only one way to be male. (Not that boundary-testing behaviour is going to vanish overnight; it even has some positive aspects, in that rules should be challenged, and gathering new knowledge may involve breaking rules.) The father of whatever sex knows quite a lot already about working co-operatively – remember, in the old language which has collapsed, she is a woman.

THE POLITICS OF PATERNAL AGGRESSION

So far, the argument has been about the more erotic side of parenting – physical warmth and recognition of the daughter as other than mother, father–son togetherness as leading to reforms in how we conceive of society itself. What about aggression, an altogether more problematic theme? Surely, some will say, only men can handle their sons' aggression?

Much depends on what we mean by 'handling' aggression. If we mean eliminating it from the picture altogether, either with discipline or by teaching stoicism in the face of frustration or adversity, we seem doomed to fail. But the question is not really how to handle, manage, discipline, or eliminate aggression; it is part of life, and it is not all bad. Rather, the task is to see how aggression might be kept moving and prevented from degenerating into destructiveness. Aggression is part of communicating. It is a valid way of securing attention. But who is to say whether an act of aggression is horribly destructive or constructively self-assertive?

As I suggested in Chapter 4, the human body can become a sort of index for aggression. Fathers rather often make use of chest aggression, exemplified by the ambivalence of the bear hug. Then there is male genital aggression exemplified by pornography. Men also go in for arm aggression, suggesting a range of images and acts from pressing a nuclear button to striking a blow with a weapon to strangling someone with bare hands. Leg aggression is often practised by fathers when they walk away and duck confrontation. Anal aggression, coming out of the bottom, involves enviously smearing the achievements of others, perhaps by snide comments – what was referred to in encounter groups as 'coming out sideways'.

The relationship between the child and the father of whatever sex is the arena in which movement between these different styles of aggression is worked on and developed. The main aim is to keep aggression fluid and moving through the various styles so as to avoid the predominance of one style over the others. When one style predominates, there is more likely to be movement from benevolent aggression to pure destructiveness. But there is more to communicating aggression between father and child than keeping several styles going at once. There is also the possibility of an element in fathering that can help to *transform* antisocial, sadistic, unrelated aggression into socially committed, self-assertive, related aggression. This transformation takes place on the social level as well as in families.

Fathers work on these issues without knowing it. For sons, the goal is to allow aggression its place in open and emotionally mobile relationships. For daughters, the goal is to validate and reinforce their capacity to challenge and fight with men. A woman's capacity to confront the patriarchy stems, to a certain extent, from the way her father played back her aggressive response to him.

As far as women who bring up daughters alone are concerned, the main thing is the need not to retreat into some spurious all-female, nicey-nicey, sisterly alliance. Lone parents usually are aware of how tempting it is for anyone who is isolated or fears rejection to do this. Equally, many women who parent alone have simply had to come to terms with an unacceptable degree of physical aggression in the family already. Perhaps lone fathers of whatever sex need to know that it may even be a good thing if they and their daughters fight. (They are going to fight at some point anyway.) This would change the terms of debate about lone-parent families and pose a few challenges for two-parent families. Fathers of whatever sex need to encourage their daughters to challenge male authority; it is often intelligent, not always disloyal, for mothers to approve of this.

There is always going to be tension and frustration in a family, and thus the possibility of aggression. But it can be reframed from the beginning as part of a relationship, not something to be eliminated. In terms of actual parenting behaviour, women who parent alone need to be reassured of what many know already: it cannot be wrong to engage in rough-and-tumble play with boys, even though such play is bound to become a bit too real from time to time. It is not always a bad thing when events get a bit out of hand – just look at the psychological damage done to people who grew up in emotionally over-controlled families, where father was certainly and perhaps simply a moral presence. What kind of training in 'handling' aggression is that?

CAN FATHERS CHANGE?

If some readers disagree that a father of whatever sex can be good-enough, they might note that it is not proven that only a male can do these things. Such readers should not forget how many men do not or cannot do them before concluding that it is impossible for a woman to do them.

Moreover, we have not yet mentioned the fact that many children living in families headed by one parent have regular contact with the other parent, or the ways in which women who parent alone can encourage contact between their children and adult males, or the part male mentors might play in some families. These issues have often been discussed.

Some readers may have less problem with women doing the fathering but do not like the idea that fathers, or men in general, can change. In fact, both the idea and the practice of fatherhood have shown incredible cross-cultural variation and changes over time; they are not written in stone. Consider the research on how fathers play with their children. Captured on video, fathers are seen to be much more active and physical, while mothers videoed playing with their children are quieter, more reflective and more protective. This result seems both logical and fixed. But if the play of fathers who, for whatever reason, have sole or primary care of their children is videoed, *it resembles that of mothers*. Fathers can change. Maybe men can change.[5]

One way in which men are changing is that they are

becoming more sceptical of the male deal described in Chapter 3. Increasingly, and especially in mid-life, men are becoming aware that repudiating everything in themselves that was soft, vulnerable, 'feminine' in exchange for receiving the desire-fulfilling goodies Western capitalism offers was not altogether a good deal after all. Among many experiences which it denied them is the experience of being a hands-on, actively involved father.

Parallels drawn between changes in the world of men and the women's movement are fallacious because of the political reality that men already possess power and resources. Nor has there yet been a radical shift in the role of the father in many households. Empirical social scientists tell us about the unchanging picture in the majority of families: most men do not look after children, do not do their share of the chores and are responsible for whatever sexual and physical abuse is perpetrated.

But the aspirational atmosphere is changing. This is very hard to measure empirically, and the intuition of a depth psychologist sometimes does not pass muster when compared to 'real' social science. I was in the United States in 1991 at the time of the Anita Hill–Clarence Thomas Congressional hearings (on the accusation of his sexual harassment of her and its impact on his nomination to the Supreme Court) and many commentators noted that the effect of these events on public consciousness was considerable. The general attack on lone-parent families and resistance to that attack may have a similar effect in many places. As political leaders have found, there are profound electoral spin-offs from paying heed to identity politics.[6] If men are changing, if we are about to see good-enough fathers in larger numbers in Western societies, then the very existence of male power takes on a new significance. If changes are taking place in the world of men and fathers, they will have political and social effects now and in the future. Throughout the book, we have seen that gender issues are especially important for politics, just as they are for therapy, because of the unique position of gender midway between the outer and inner worlds. Both our public *and* our private lives are riddled with gender issues. Indeed, one way of understanding the unending wave of sex scandals in British and American politics is to see them as highlighting the shakiness and shifting nature of our present images of masculinity, and the problems we are having trying to work out what are and are not acceptable modes of behaviour for men.[7]

People living in lone-parent families have become experts at living with the changes in gender role that are sweeping over the Western world. Could we reframe lone parents and their children as today's experts at coping with changes that threaten to drive everyone crazy by their depth and rapidity? The attack on lone parents in many Western countries has presented us with an opportunity to inject psychological realism and sensitivity into our politics, acknowledging that the old politics, which sought to leave out personal experience, are falling to pieces. People living in lone-parent families may be the expert practitioners of this new kind of psychological politics. Can we learn from them?

PSYCHOTHERAPY AND THE FATHER

Although Winnicott coined the phrase 'the good-enough mother' in 1949, the good-enough *father* has not been written about very much.[8, 9] Yet retheorizing the father is necessary if psychoanalysis is to progress beyond a politically biased image of the father that reflects a specific historical and social period in Western culture. When Winnicott disputes the seriousness for a small baby of having a psychotic *father* (as opposed to a psychotic mother) or when he speaks of the father showing his gun to his children as a way of explaining what the outer world is like, his work reeks of cultural and historical contingency.[10] Yet psychoanalysis worldwide continues to offer what I call the 'insertion metaphor' as the root image of the father's penetrative, unwavering psychological role in a child's early life. The father of early childhood is supposed to insert himself, like a giant depriving and separating penis, between mother and baby, who would otherwise stay locked in a psychosis-inducing and phase-inappropriate symbiosis. In Margaret Mahler's psychoanalytic account, the father awakens a 2 year old from sleep and turns that child towards the (or is it his?) world.[11]

This comforting but reactionary story about fathers – father holding mother who holds baby (with its avoidance of the detail of a more direct relationship with children) – is one that urgently requires critique, not least because of the insult to mothers and babies contained in the notion that they have no commitment and capacities in themselves to becoming separate. Do mothers and babies really want to be psychotic? Moreover, what is so wonderful about the rupture of the mother–child relationship depicted by psychoanalysis, together with rapture over the strong ego that is supposed to result, a question well-posed by feminist theorists on both sides of the Atlantic?[12]

Jacques Lacan's work does focus on the father and in it we find a dematerialization of the father so complete that he crops up in accounts of development solely as a metaphor.

Father is a name or Name in a complicated psychoanalytic theorem; a third term relation to the mother–infant dyad. We should note that, even in Lacan's work, father and child are never really regarded as in immediate relationship. This approach fails to recognize the interplay between the father's concrete, literal presence and his metaphorical function.[13] For Lacan, as John Forrester says, 'the father's function is *strictly metaphorical* – he functions neither as real father (flesh and blood) nor as imaginary father (though he later figures in fantasy as an ideal or punitive agency).'[14] Is it really possible to divorce the literal and the metaphorical as Lacan does, either for purposes of description or as a mode of understanding? All of Lacan's abstractions about the phallus cannot do away with the fleshy actuality of the father's penis as the raw material from which the metaphor has fashioned itself.

Lacan was as culture bound as anyone else. Could a conscious recognition of the positive, direct, physical, affirming father–infant relationship, dating from the earliest moment, have been possible either in the bourgeois France of Lacan's childhood (he was born in 1901) or during his adult life of psychoanalytic theory-making?

What of C. G. Jung and the post-Jungians? As he sought to identify the essential and invariant features of father–child relationships – the so-called father archetype or archetypal father – Jung overlooked the way in which such relationships are built in culture. But if we do explore the father–child relation, we see that, in most cultures, it is dependent on the intersection of two other relationships: that between mother and child, and that between woman and man. A man does not become a father in either a formal or an emotional sense unless something happens simultaneously within the space created by these other two relationships. What that 'some-thing' is, and what the father does, varies from culture to culture and across time. (Actually, the way that the father–child relationship is constructed is no different from the mother–child relationship, which, as many writers have argued, is not as natural, biological, innate, ahistorical, uni-versal and 'given' as we used to think.)[15]

FATHERS IN FUTURE

Realizing that the father is a culturally constructed creature leads to all kinds of possibilities. The father relation cannot be approached via absolute definition; it is a situational and relative matter. So a new judgement is required on what may seem like hopelessly idealistic and utopian attempts to change the norms of the father's role. The father's role can change, because written into it is the refusal of absolute defi-nition. This refusal is made possible by male political power and freedom and by the historical and cultural mutability of the father relation. Hence, the only 'archetypal' aspect of the father is that there is no archetypal aspect.

If there is no father archetype of the kind that would hold us back, what can *we* do to help the process of change along? It is still hard to find accounts of the father that depict his benevolent aspects as opposed to his undeniably malevolent ones. Very little has been said about the father's potential to contribute to the political and psychological mobility, en-franchisement and emancipation of others.

Here are some areas in which psychotherapists might con-tribute to new social and political thinking about the father:

- ❖ changing the social expectation that only women will look after small babies
- ❖ fostering a culture in which parenthood and work may coexist
- ❖ working towards more co-operative and less hierarchical forms of political and social organization
- ❖ getting a clearer understanding of male sexuality in general and paternal sexuality in particular (partly to be able to do more effective work with problems such as child sexual abuse)
- ❖ changing how we define and what we expect from good-enough families to include lone-parent families and other transgressive modes of family life.

Traditionally, the father is not only the locus and source of power in the family (and, hence, in society) but also the parent who radiates and deals in spirituality. This is, of course, another kind of power. The spiritual realm, like that of gender, is a liminal one, straddling the divide between 'higher' and 'lower' or between 'transcendent' and 'earthbound'. Like gender, spirituality generates its own special politics, and these form the spine of the next chapter.

CHAPTER EIGHT

Politics, spirituality, psychotherapy

'SPIRITUALITY' IS a very vague word. A recent topic of debate between philosophers revolves around the concept of 'vagueness'.[1] Some philosophers would suggest that, instead of moaning or making jokes about defining elephants, we accept the inevitability of vagueness for a discussion of spirituality, rejecting the spurious precision that dominates the style and content of so many contemporary discourses.

Spirituality may be rooted in traditional, formal religion. Or it may be a highly idiosyncratic and personal affair. Or both. Spirituality may be located above us, at ground level (even in the body) or below, in an underworld. Or on all three levels. Spirituality may be understood as universal, comprehensive and catholic with a small 'c'. Or it may be experienced and expressed radically differently according to time, place, age, sex, sexual orientation, ethnicity, class and one's physical and psychological health. Or both. Spirituality may be regarded as beyond the transpersonal, transcending the human realms of existence. Or it may exist only in a relational, intersubjective, interactional setting. Or both. Spirituality may be seen as a substance or essence – breath, pneuma, ruach. Or it may be more of a perspective on experience. Or both.

How can something like spirituality be apprehended except in its relation to its opposite? But what is its opposite? Is it the body, the social, the secular, the profane, the soul, the psychological – or what?

This chapter explores three sides of a coin: spirituality, psychotherapy and political issues of social justice. While approaches to psychotherapy and counselling that are specifically and avowedly 'spiritual' certainly still exist, there has been a tendency since the late 1970s to omit the spiritual dimension from mainstream, rigorous, professional therapy work. Similarly, psychotherapy and politics, and politics and spirituality, are usually kept apart. But connectedness between human beings is surely both spiritual and political.

There is no intention on my part of collapsing spirituality, psychotherapy and politics into each other: we should always be suspicious of cheap holism as a response to complex problems. But the way in which the borderlines and boundaries between spirituality, psychotherapy and politics have been positioned requires challenge. Hillel, the first-century Jewish sage, captured the urgency of this when he wrote: 'If I am not for myself, who is for me? If I am only for myself, what am I? And if not now, when?'

THE PLURAL SPIRIT

The focus will be in turn on social spirituality, democratic spirituality, craft spirituality, profane spirituality and spiritual sociality.

The concept of *social spirituality* stems from Jewish traditions (just as psychoanalysis does). It is not simply a question of discovering oneself as a spiritual being and going out and meeting other people who are already spiritual beings. It is a question of going out and meeting people and, together with those other people, becoming spiritual beings by doing something together. That is what *Tikkun*, restoration and repair of the world, implies: one achieves spirituality in part by being a certain kind of human being in society. But where is the psychological underpinning for this type of Jewish-inspired social spirituality?

Here, we may turn to Jung, not so much for his specific theories on the subject, but, as so often, for his intuitive suggestions about *how* to start to do something, not *what* to do in precise terms.

Jung introduced the idea of the psychoid level of the unconscious, where psyche and matter are two sides of a coin. A new but related notion of 'the spiritoid' refers us to a level of spiritual experience where the spiritual and the social comingle. If the transpersonal, spiritual dimensions of life exist in society and are therefore staring us in the face all the time, we do not really need a separate strand of transpersonal psychology or transpersonal philosophy. The transpersonal is always there in society already, at the spiritoid level, where spirituality and sociality merge. The problem is that we failed to notice this. Everything that ends in politics starts in mysticism.

Clinically, too, the spiritual is often hidden in the open. I was once consulted by a young mental health professional called Michael, who came to see me because of his obsessive thoughts about the nature of life after death. If there was nothing after death, then what possible joy or satisfaction could there be in life? What I heard was that his father, and many other members of his family, were in a kind of spiritual void. They had come from religious backgrounds with which all of them, not just the client, had lost contact. What was so interesting to watch and witness was not only the client engaging with neurosis by getting in touch with his own lost religious self (as Jung depicted it), but also his realization that his task was – with their active co-operation – to re-religionize or resacralize his family. He set out to do it with, it has to be said, mixed results. He lacked appropriate rites and sacraments. But the task was perhaps the important thing for Michael, rather than his success in achieving it.

The second in this plurality of spiritualities was *democratic spirituality*. Jung and James Hillman have mounted a challenge to the ever-upwards out-of-the-world habits of the Western spirit. They have urged us to think about the downwards, darkening, deepening move into soul. But there are problems with these images of upwardness (spirit) and of downwardness (soul) because both have become romanticized, both have become elitist. It is already the case that people feel they are supposed to move upwards or downwards, in certain prescribed ways.

Rather, spirituality holds out the hope of something crucial to democracy; it may be the last arena in which equality, or equality of potential, can exist (the last usually denied by contemporary social and political theorists on scientific grounds: genetics, intelligence testing, the supposedly inevitable inequality in the distribution of ability). Spiritual potential is something quite other than educational potential or vocational potential or relational potential. Since it is not susceptible to measurement, equality is its precondition, its *sine qua non* and not an outcome. There really is no spiritual equivalent to how many times a night you can do it or how many degrees you have or how much you earn. The notion of spiritual potential enables us to think in terms of equality of outcome.

The third spirituality I mentioned was a *craft spirituality*, which locates holiness in the artificiality of the made world, the manufactured world – the atelier or even the factory. In modernity, whether it is called late modernism or post-capitalism or Fordism, the main strands are industrialization and technology: the making of things. This is still the case in the VDU world of post-modernity; things are made – even services are made. In modern life, there is a holiness waiting to be released. The roots of holiness, on this reading of it, do not only lie in God, or in the transpersonal realm. They also lie in our making or manufacture of holiness: holiness as artifice. We make holiness all the time by conceiving of, designing and constructing sacred spaces, which used to be called temples. We make and manufacture holiness when we perform certain acts – sacred or even profane acts – such as sacrificial acts, or acts of repentance, or acts of creativity, or even acts of bodily self-indulgence and self-abuse. Holiness can be made by humans, and hence be supremely artificial.

The notion that holiness is to be found in the material and social world is not a new one. For many people, whether religious or non-religious, the material world has long had this gleam to it. Since my childhood I have been fascinated by God's detailed instructions to the Children of Israel about how to build the Ark of the Covenant, and the Tabernacle (or Noah's Ark earlier on). Let us consider for a moment the Ark of the Covenant, that portable sanctuary, symbol of holy manufacture, and allow it to become a metaphor in our discussion. In the divine instructions for the construction of this Ark, what do we see? First of all, that God is the most tremendous obsessional fusspot. But we also see how ineffable holiness really does depend on every detail, every joint, every bevel, every dimension, and the kinds of materials that are used to make holiness:

> And Bezaleel made the ark of shittim wood. Two cubits and a half was the length of it, and a cubit and a half the breadth of it, and a cubit and a half the height of it. And he overlaid it with pure gold within and without, and made a crown of gold to it round about. And he cast for it four rings of gold, to be set by the four corners of it; even two rings upon the one side of it, and two rings upon the other side of it. And he made staves of shittim wood, and overlaid them with gold. And he put the staves into the rings by the side of the ark to bear the ark.[2]

What happened to Bezaleel? Where is our Bezaleel consciousness today? Why do we have so few portable tabernacles? Where is our capacity to recognize that holiness is not only God-made, not only natural, and not only made by us humans, but also there for the making? Idolatry lurks as the shadow of craft spirituality, but only things of substance cast a shadow.

The next category of spirituality was *profane spirituality*. Here is a short quote from Zaehner's book *Mysticism Sacred and Profane*: 'There is no point at all in blinking at the fact that the raptures of the theistic mystic are closely akin to the transports of sexual union.'[3] The idea that sex is often numinous need not be dwelt upon too long; that sex is sometimes frightening is probably self-evident also. But what kind of sexuality lends itself to mysticism and spiritual projects?

Jung pointed out that, for members of the same family to get into deep intimate contact, there has to be something that stops them from turning away from each other. Something that makes it impossible for the people in the family to

avoid one another – a vehicle, a motor, a generator for intimacy and love. Jung suggested that incestuous sexual fantasy
helps people to get into a situation where they cannot avoid
one another. At a deeper level, inside the family and probably
outside it as well, this is what being 'turned on' is about. In
the family there is an appropriate dimension of sexual excitation which leads to personality-enhancing interactions
between people, and, out of these, spiritual connections are
fashioned.

But this perspective also applies beyond the family.
Profane spirituality implies that the purpose or aim of
sexual arousal is something more than reproduction or dis-
charge of the drive. There is something that goes beyond
the unending psychoanalytic exploration of the vicissitudes
of desire in the unconscious – a more teleological aspect to
incestuous sexuality, whose *telos* is spirit. Hence, spirit also
plays a part in bringing people into relationships where
they cannot avoid each other: in the family and in social life
generally. The benign fetishism of human sexual arousal
and excitation lies at the heart of what I am calling profane
spirituality: when it has to be that one person, the special
one, and no other will do. Profane spirituality involves
more than sex, whether we think of incestuous sex or sex
outside the family. There are also questions of drugs and
alcohol. We need to look at these psychopathologies as spiritual matters. Writing to the founder of Alcoholics Anony-
mous, Jung made the point that there is an off-the-rails
spiritual search involved in alcoholism. Similarly, there is a
spiritual as well as a materialistic dimension to drug addic-
tion, the use of tobacco and maybe also to shopping and
consumerism, if one knows where to look for it. Spirituality
is not only a matter of maturity or individuation; it also

resides in confusion, suffering and immaturity. The gods have become symptoms, said Jung.

Importantly, profane spirituality is contemporary spirituality: popular music, sport, fashion all exert a power akin to that of religious or mystical experience. It is time to recognize that the spirituality in our world, our manufactured and made spirituality, our craft spirituality, is oozing out of the profane pores of contemporary life. It only needs us to recognize and name it. In Bani Shorter's words, everything is susceptible to the sacred.[4]

Lastly, we turn to *spiritual sociality*. Briefly, this concerns the latent spirituality in organizations, whether community organizations or economic organizations, such as co-operatives, trade unions and the like, teams of all kinds, the manifold groupings and networks of civic society. All these things partake in a certain kind of spiritualized ritual process.

THE HIDDEN SPIRITUAL POLITICS OF HUMAN CONNECTEDNESS

Most of us have inherited a particular vision of how people relate to one another in society: split-up and atomized individuals have to struggle to get into relationships with each other. According to psychoanalysis, this occurs via projections and introjections. The ceaseless play of movement from inside to outside and back again implies that individuals are regarded as first positioned in empty space, that is that there is nothing between us to start with.

Could we imagine instead something like a 'social ether', which connects people from the beginning? There would then be no empty space between people, though it may look as if there were. Physicists tell us that 98 per cent of the universe is composed of cold dark matter, which definitely exists even if no one has been able to locate or measure it. This is a reassuring statement from my point of view because it refutes the idea that people are physically separate, and hence the notion that we have to struggle to achieve relatedness. Psychoanalysis might then be completely wrong about how relationships arise. Moreover, there is no reason or need to postulate a struggle to separate if being un-separate is an ordinary state of affairs and not a pathology. This un-separateness is quintessentially spiritual.

Psychoanalysis, trading off the Western notion of an autonomous self, has encouraged us to place separation at the top of a hierarchy or scale of psychological values. But being jointly immersed in the social ether, one with another, need not be an immature or neurotic or psychotic state. There is actually no basis for privileging the bloody struggle towards the kind of autonomous, atomized, de-spiritualized individualistic self that Western societies have espoused, and which is now beginning to poison them.

Another heuristic image for social relations is that of a rhizome, the nutrient tube under the ground out of which stalks come up through the surface of the earth. In a garden, these stalks look separate. But our knowledge about what is going on below the surface tells us that they share a non-visible root-base. One way of looking at some formal psychological theories of connectedness, such as the collective unconscious, is to regard them as examples of a hidden, rhizomic, spiritual tradition of connectedness in Western culture.

Consider the rhizomic language of feminist psychotherapeutic and psychological thinking: Susie Orbach's 'separated attachment', for example, or the title of a book of papers from the Stone Center in America – *Women's Growth in Connection*. Or Carol Gilligan's work, where she disputes that all morality is principled and abstract morality, and writes about a morality of care based on relational values. These phrases and emphases are further indications of a tradition very different from the individualistic version of humanity. Yet the tradition of primary connectedness has somehow been suppressed or defeated in the West, and modern psychotherapy has, for the most part, colluded in this.

In contemporary Western politics, one ubiquitous yet problematic word is 'community'. Political thinkers speak of a traditional sense of pulling together that used to exist and is now lost. The loss is felt keenly. For other theorists, the idea of community is more proactive, referring to a new kind of egalitarian politics based on their belief in what is shared, held in common, faced together.

In the heated discussions about community that are taking place, little room has been made for a psychological contribution. But a community-based politics requires an overtly socialized psychology that will also need to be a transpersonal psychology. Politics is itself a transpersonal activity and hence politics points in a spiritual direction. Psychotherapy is not a religion, though it may be the heir to some aspects of conventional religion. Factoring the psychological into the political seems to require religious language. Perhaps this is because psychotherapy, politics and religion all share, at some level, in the fantasy of providing healing for the world. (The very word 'fantasy' may create problems for some readers. But fantasy is not in itself pathological. There is a necessarily utopic role for fantasy in political discourse.)

In a sense, psychotherapy functions as a new monasticism. Just as the monks and nuns kept culture in Europe alive

during the so-called 'Dark Ages', so, too, in their equally rigorous way, therapists and analysts are keeping something
alive in our own age. However, the values that psychotherapy
keeps alive are difficult to classify. They do not have the ring
of absolute Truth (though such a possibility is not ruled
out); nor are they based on a fixed account of human nature
(though that is what is invariably being attempted). In its
discovery of values and value in that which other disciplines
reject, psychotherapy helps to keep something alive in the
face of threats ranging from state hegemony to vicious
market forces to nostalgic longings for a mythical past in
which certitudes about nation, gender and race provide stability.

We often hear calls for placing a global ethic or a global
sense of responsibility into the heart of political theory and
the political process. How can this be done without some
kind of psychological sensitivity and awareness? This sensitivity and awareness may not be easily measurable by the
sturdy tools of empiricism, but instead reveal themselves in
dream, in parental and primal scene imagery, in an understanding of the individual's political history, development
and myth. Hence, clinical work on oneself coexists with
political work in one's society.

PSYCHOTHERAPY AND THE SENSE OF JUSTICE

What is justice in this post-modern, multicultural, relativis-
tic, socially constructed world, devoid as it is of eternal or
even humanistic values or grand narratives? What is justice
after the death of God? In Greek times, even the gods were
subject to justice, which meant that justice had no location.

Then the Judaeo-Christian tradition developed, and started to locate justice in heaven – somewhere else than in the social world here on earth. At that point, a split began to develop between spiritual values and what we would now call social theory. We can heal that split by positioning psychology and psychotherapy somewhere between spiritual values, such as equality in God's eyes, on the one hand, and social theories of equality on the other.

It is commonplace for social theorists to regard the concept of equality in God's eyes as pre-modern, and to see it as having justified all manner of earthly inequalities, thereby reinforcing the status quo in oppressive societies. This is not unreasonable, as the record shows. But it is an incomplete reading, because even in modern accounts of social justice and equality, the notion of an ineluctable psycho-spiritual equality bubbles beneath the surface as a kind of positive shadow. (The relationship between Christianity and socialism in Britain is one example of the general pattern.)

Consider John Rawls's classic work on justice, *A Theory of Justice*.[5] This book has set the tone for most major debates about social justice ever since its publication. Without attempting to summarize Rawls's views in detail, I want to suggest that one of the most significant contemporary philosophers of social justice has pushed his thinking into the areas that spirituality and psychotherapy inhabit. It behoves us to listen to what the intersection of Rawlsian ideas about justice and therapeutic work might tell us.

Rawls discusses the distribution of goods in society, how it cannot be absolutely fair yet should be fair enough. He accepts that we can have an unequal distribution of things like money or power, provided that people who are less well off are specially catered for. By all means have inequalities, as long as they are part of a greater move towards a general less-ening of inequality.

Implicit in Rawls's discussion is the idea that self-esteem and mutual respect are goods that can be distributed within a society. They are not only psychological qualities present or not present in and between individuals but goods to be dis-tributed in societies. We could then have a psychologically inflected debate about how we might distribute or redistrib-ute self-esteem and mutual respect in British society. If that debate were to begin, psychotherapists could be, should be part of it. After all, they know about the personal constraints, delimiters and parameters on the growth of self-esteem and mutual respect. It is their stock in trade.

However, there could hardly be any noticeable redistribu-tion of self-esteem and mutual respect without redistribu-tion also in its more usual sense – in the economic sphere. Hence, the next chapter concerns economics.

CHAPTER NINE

The economic psyche

WHY ECONOMICS?

Why is a focus on economics so important to a psychologically inflected approach to today's politics? A friend said, 'Nobody will dispute that economics is important, but everyone will offer different reasons for it.'

The first reason – and the most compelling one, naive as it sounds – is an ethical one. Because of economic thinking and economic systems people are suffering and dying every day. Anyone with a conscience has to try to evaluate what is going on in the economic sphere.

Second, economics is extraordinarily influential on all of us. Paul Samuelson, Nobel laureate and writer of the most widely used standard text on economics, said, 'Let those who will write the nation's laws, just so long as I can write its economics textbooks.' In the 1930s John Maynard Keynes made the claim that 'Practical men who believe themselves to be quite exempt from any intellectual influences, are usually the slaves of some defunct economist.' Economics exerts an extremely powerful influence. But in spite of the fantastic changes in economic behaviour, organization and thinking over the past 250 years, citizens are all too often supposed to believe in today's preferred economic theory as if it were written in stone.

The third reason for discussing economics in this book has to do with credibility. A psychotherapist who spends a good deal of time and earns most of his money doing clinical work is trying to say something about the wider world of politics. People crossing disciplinary boundaries are going to find their credibility called into question, and economics is a difficult topic anyway. So let me confess at the outset that, when it comes to economics, most psychotherapists do not pass muster if they allow the professional economists to set the agenda. Yet no matter how unworldly psychotherapists seem to be, if they show an interest in economics, and have something to say about it, politicians tend to listen, at least initially. It is a viable way to enter the political arena, more viable than making statements about gender or environmentalism or conflict resolution. Economic issues, such as class, are still the hard-edged, down-to-earth, real world themes of our times.

RETRAINING THE PSYCHE

In my workshops on the 'economic psyche', participants are asked to imagine what would happen if they were told their jobs were about to be eliminated for some reason. What other kinds of jobs could they do? What new skills would they need? How long do they think it would take to become competent in a new field of work?

Probably most of us know someone whose employment is threatened by technological innovation, international competition or cultural shifts. (With the advent of so many psychotropic drugs, psychotherapists are also susceptible to such pressures.) That is why the exercise produces such extraordinarily powerful emotional responses, with people from many different backgrounds breaking down in tears. Political commentators have noted that, in the West, the well-known employment problems of male factory workers whose rustbelt industries are moribund are just one aspect of a global transformation in labour economics. In countries like Britain and the United States, the fear of vocational extinction has spread deep into the middle classes. When social stresses hit the middle classes, the world is going to hear about it! These are not people in traditionally disempowered groups. They are people like those who might be reading this book.

No one can any longer assume that they have a job for life; in the course of a working life, each of us is going to have many jobs. This means our employability will be directly dependent on our adaptability and flexibility. We will have to convince employers, and tell ourselves, that we can learn, meaning we can learn *on the job*. Adaptability and flexibility at work are, of course, psychological characteristics and hence subject to all the usual psychological vicissitudes.

A conference organized in London in 1994 by a Labour Party think-tank on training and retraining for work was addressed by the then US labor secretary Robert Reich and Labour's then shadow chancellor of the exchequer Gordon Brown. They told us that we are entering the age of education-driven economics: training and retraining, they said, are the keys to a successful modern economy. The huge collective psychological changes being demanded were addressed in a casual manner. Actually, the emotional impact of perpetually retraining for successive different jobs in the course of a lifetime was not truly addressed at all. But if these proposals, paralleled in other Western countries and supported by many opinion formers and policy makers, are not to be defeated by massive passive – or active – resistance, attention will need to be paid to the collective psychological dimension.

What Reich and Brown referred to as the 'permanent educational revolution' in the world of work is going to affect women and men differently. It is not that women and men have inherently different psychological make-ups which express themselves totally differently in the world of work. Rather, the rigidly inscribed arrangements by which the genders are organized make it likely that men and women will react differently to the new economic regime that is being proposed and that will probably emerge.

Many women are likely to feel that they are already displaying the kind of economic flexibility these politicians are advocating: they are already entering and leaving the world of work as they respond to society's demands to fulfil their so-called female role as carers for children. Yet most countries do not really reward flexibility, and many do not even facilitate it. Being flexible at work often means being low-paid – it is a specific example of the worldwide problem of the feminization of poverty, by which women (and hence children) bear the brunt of recession and economic dislocation.

Women have spoken and written eloquently about the balancing acts they have to perform to keep all their various social roles in psychological harmony. Of course, the result is not always harmonious, and many women realize that the approved goal of achieving an integration of all their roles and a settled, single identity is just part of Rivière's 'female masquerade',[1] a stratagem that many women have to deploy for themselves to avoid the psychological tensions between social oneness and social manyness.

So it is not at all certain that women will rush to embrace the new labour economics of Messrs Reich and Brown. At the conference, there was altogether too much of a top-down rather than a bottom-up approach. These new strategies for re-employment do not show much respect for women's indigenous knowledge. How do women remake themselves time and time again? Are the (male) politicians going to try to find out?

At the workshops, one thing that we have experimented with is what it feels like to start to train oneself to do a new job well before the old job is played out – a kind of constructively schizoid attitude to work. Women's life narratives about flexibility have been a useful source of mentoring for men here. Something else that has become clear is that training is more effective when it is placed within a generally enriching framework and not confined to precise techniques learned and applied at the workplace. What the politicians consider to be 'education' may be psychologically demeaning. There is no reason in principle why work should not be a form of self-expression, but we have to make a start by treating it as such. If education becomes too work-oriented, its capacity to release people's potential will be stunted.

For men, the problems with the new labour economics are more psychologically intense and more likely to lead to a political impasse. Yet it ought to be possible for men to go beyond what has been called 'victim envy' to see what can be done about the changes in the workplace that are affecting them psychologically. There are special problems for unskilled men in localities where traditional industries have vanished. Far from having jobs for life, they face life with nary a job in sight. Their grasp on authority, power and dignity is removed, and many bear emotional scars. If you cannot rely on what you know today being true and useful tomorrow, your whole world-view is undermined.

In many respects, the Reich-Brown recipe fits perfectly into a cultural milieu in the West in which male supremacy in the political, social and economic spheres is being challenged from a number of quarters. One could scarcely say that the challenge has been very successful as yet, and the backlash certainly *was* effective, but the way in which social and cultural issues related to masculinity (violence, sexual abuse, job insecurity, the backlash against feminism) have forced their way on to the political agenda since 1990 is striking.

When men have to admit that there is no door-opening knowledge to which they have special access, they face a full-frontal psychological onslaught on their dominant position in culture. How will they react to what many of them experience as an economic plague? Often, their sense of betrayal leads them to look for scapegoats. But the feeling of betrayal is more profound than can be assuaged by blaming feminists or rioting in the inner city. What is being betrayed is the false promise of masculinity itself.

There is something at stake here in terms of the evolution of Western consciousness. We are witnessing a redefining by politicians who have not thought through what we understand by knowledge and skill. They are seeking to retrain the psyche. In the long term, the unmanning of work may bring all manner of benefits to the community – which is not to deny the short-term emotional hell that many men will go through. For women, while the hell may be the one they know already, it will be particularly galling to see what gains they have achieved being swept away, not by simplistic men's movement gurus, but by the inexorable collective power of man-centred economic forces. Women, too, will want to explore what work could come to mean in the twenty-first century. For both women and men, then, gender issues will be at the heart of key economic debates in the years ahead. And that means that psychology will play a part, too. The personal is not only political – but also economic.

THE NEW DEBATE

If we accept that the personal is economic, then many aspects of economics can be understood from a psychological perspective. For example, from the standpoint of both psychology and politics, the old debate between the free marketeers and those who espouse a government-planned economy is played out. Despite electoral slogans, nobody in positions of influence is emotionally invested in either extreme position any more, although much progressive political energy is still being wasted in rectitudinous diatribes against the free market. But numerous books have now been written to show that what we thought was a free market in the neo-liberal heyday of the 1980s was nothing of the sort. Nor will people ever enjoy a free market in the Eastern European countries or the Third World. This debate about the free market has simply fizzled out. Even on the right, the issue is framed in terms of restricting 'big' government or 'cutting' entitlements – the idealization of no government at all and virtually no taxes could not be sustained.

Nevertheless, we still need to explore the psychology of

the market economy because, whether it exists or not, it has become a worldwide numinous image. To say that the market economy is numinous means that, as an image, an idea, a catchphrase, it has deeply captivated people whether they wanted to be captivated or not. When something numinous enters the picture, things get polarized. The polarization about the market economy was plain for everyone to see: on one side were those who believed that the market economy is the only economic system that works and is the guarantor of freedom, liberty and democracy. On the other side were those who saw the market and its ruthlessness as lying behind the despoliation of the planet, the exploitation of women and children and the gradual erosion of the future for our descendants.

When confronted with two such extreme verdicts on the same complicated socioeconomic phenomenon – the market economy – what were we to do? We had to choose, or we felt we had to. This psychologically exciting compulsion has blinded us to the more sober fact that the debate about the market is politically moribund. Intellectually, most of us probably knew already that we had contradictory feelings about the free market. On the one hand, it did often seem to generate resources, to be productive in the broadest sense. On the other hand – and we looked at Republican America or Conservative Britain when we said this – it did seem, also inevitably, to lead to social destruction, waste of resources, unfairness and a kind of moral anarchy.

What has taken the life and energy away from the debates about market- or government-planned economies has been the emergence of a new set of economic ideas and policies different from both those espoused by the free marketeers and those espoused by advocates of a planned economy. The knowledge and concepts of psychotherapy can be usefully employed to evaluate the viability, realism and creativity of these new economic ideas, and their potential contribution to achieving social justice.

The dominant alternative economic idea currently being put forward concerns sustainable development or sustainable growth. Its basic premise is that, living on a bounded planet, we should not use resources we cannot replace. We should use only resources that we can replace within a realistic time-frame. The problem with the idea of sustainable development is that, if we work it out statistically, we have to conclude that the whole world should function economically at approximately the level of Portugal in 1950. Some would say that is not so terrible. Others are plain horrified at such authoritarian idealism.

Another alternative economic idea has to do with a redistribution of wealth between the countries of North and South, an attempt to reverse the present situation wherein, because of debt and interest repayments, there is actually a capital flow from the poorer countries to the richer countries, from the underdeveloped to the overdeveloped. This was certainly not the goal of international aid policies since the 1960s, but it is their outcome. Hence, alternative economic thinkers stress that *our* relative affluence is achieved at the expense of *their* relative poverty, and that rich and poor worldwide are psychologically linked by such financial and economic processes. Such an idea is anathema to free marketeers.

A third piece of alternative economic thinking has to do with its pronounced commitment to environmentalist principles. One particularly radical idea – radical in that it transcends the notion of ownership – is that there are what might be called global commons. These include the atmosphere, the oceans and those parts of the planet that have not yet been thoroughly settled, such as the Arctic and Antarctic Circles. Albeit the most provocative and difficult to assimilate, this is one of a whole range of environmentalized economic concepts that inform alternative economists' thinking on problems like pollution or the greenhouse effect.

A fourth alternative economic idea is that special attention needs to be paid to the situation of women in the present-day economies of the West because of the increased feminization of poverty. As noted earlier, women suffer disproportionately at times of recession and benefit relatively less in times of economic recovery. It used to be thought that this phenomenon occurred only in the Third World, but now it is absolutely clear that it happens in Western countries as well. Since 1980, women, and hence children, who are not in the affluent one-third of society, have got poorer more rapidly than men.

Finally, in terms of power, the new economic thinking struggles to achieve a better balance, a more workable balance, between the global, national, local and individual levels of power.

What all this adds up to is a huge shift in values – a profound, complex, nearly unbearable, perhaps doomed-to-fail psychological shift in our philosophies of life, which has powerful implications for the way we live. It means a quality-of-life retrenchment. It means a partial disavowal of the idea of economic progress.

Are these alternative economic ideas that I have sketched out psychologically and politically realistic and feasible? The answer is: yes and no. They are not realistic and feasible in the sense that they could be adopted immediately, easily or practically. It is also very difficult to see at first glance how human greed, competitiveness and love of the good life can in any way be disciplined or turned back. At the same time, this thinking and the values that inform it are already penetrating into surprising places. For several reasons, business corporations are starting to think about decentralization. The civil services of the West consider how to tax polluters and, following the Earth Summit in Rio in 1992 and its follow-up meetings, alternative economics is getting into governnmental discourse. At the moment, this influence is mostly at the level of reports, documents, think-tanks, committees and the like. But who knows? After the immense controversy surrounding the 1999 meeting of the World Trade Organization in Seattle, it may go on to find a wider political acceptance. Tellingly, a best-selling economic book in Britain and the United States in 1993–4 was called *Alternative Economic Indicators*; even within the economics profession, bastion of resistance to ideas about sustainable development, there is a recognition that we could perhaps look for alternative ways to measure the good life.

It is these ideas that have rendered the old pro- or anti-market debate redundant. A new and equally intense debate has begun to emerge. Its psychological intricacies can be clearly discerned in both the United States and Britain, where it is being carried on between what we might call the modified marketeers (exemplified by the Clinton and Blair administrations) and the alternative economists whose views have just been summarized. The debate picks up on the tension between feasibility and idealism that has caused so much trouble for the Green parties and for environmental politics generally. Whether or not such parties should join in coalition governments has become a key question for Green politicians in several European countries. Often individuals – economists or plain citizens – will experience this psychological tension within themselves.

The modified marketeers aim at a 'social market', meaning an economic system that provides a degree of governmental regulation of business and finance plus a safety net for those who are struggling. They are interested in increasing productivity via government encouragement of investment in new technology and equipment and extensive retraining programmes, though they have some 'green' sensibilities about pollution and so forth. The modified marketeers believe that the system can be made to work better, that is in a way that combines efficiency and social justice. We see modified marketeers not only in the Labour Party, in the Clinton administration and in American politics generally, but also in the Western European social democratic parties, in ruling circles in Eastern Europe and sometimes even in the emergent economies of the Pacific rim. They are strong on realism and relatively weak on value change. The alternative economists, on the other hand, following E.F. Schumacher ('small is beautiful'), are weaker on realism and strong on value change, having many interesting and challenging things to say about the way we live, especially in the West, today.

Alternative economists are devoted to changing our values and the way these inform thinking about economics. They are not interested in productivity but prefer, following a wide range of ecologistic or environmentalist philosophies, to explore dismantling the industrial infrastructures in pursuit of sustainable development and a more just economic and trade balance between the countries of North and South. They want to decentralize economic activity, they try to respect local knowledge and ways of doing things (change seen as coming from below) and are challenging conventional wisdom by, for example, experimenting with local currency schemes in which ordinary money is not used. Believing that work is a form of self-expression and self-creation, they are also interested in areas such as retraining, but for quite different reasons from those of the modified marketeers: not only to enhance productivity, but also for an enhancement of the quality of life. Similarly, the environmentalism of the alternative economists goes far beyond the greening of production methods sought by the modified marketeers.

Now, it is not necessary to agree totally with this depiction of this debate (although various politicians and economists in the United States and Britain have done so, confirming my sense that many of us feel torn in just this way). The point is that it is a *debate between progressives* – between individuals and groups whose hearts are *all* in the right place! Those who advocate feasibility, programmes for economic regeneration and recovery and so forth, are not somehow less moral or less full of integrity than those who call for a complete shift in world-view and the dismantling of capitalism altogether. A good deal of attention has been paid by the modified marketeers to rendering the market more compassionate, to tenderizing it, creating capitalism with a human face. But what if we were to switch the emphasis to toughening the alternative economists, by subjecting these resacralizers to coexistence with the more dispassionate modified marketeers? There is everything to play for, provided the men and women of vision access their reserves of realism and the men and women of realism access their reserves of vision.

PSYCHOLOGICAL ECONOMICS

Feasibility and idealism – can they ever be brought together in human affairs generally, and in the economic sphere in particular? This is, fundamentally, a psychological question. We can introduce psychology to economics via the psycho-analytic concept of ambivalence that has been mentioned throughout this book. Ambivalence about the debate in economics between modified marketeers and alternative economics does not mean our trying to combine or synthesize the best features of the two approaches. That cannot be a satisfactory solution, since something central to each would necessarily get lost. But what if each economic philosophy were to be allowed to develop in its own particular way? What might happen then?

We could begin by stating openly that, while we do not want *rich capitalists*, with all the destructiveness and inequality they bring, we do want *wealth-creating entrepreneurs*, with all the social benefits that their productivity undeniably brings. We want the entrepreneurs because they do in fact create wealth. We do not want them to become very rich capitalists (even if they want to) because that leads to the kind of unfair, death-dealing, planet-despoiling system we do not like. How could we get to a situation in which there were entrepreneurs who did not become capitalists? Could we rescue the idea of the market from capitalism in some way?

We could limit the permitted turnover of private companies headed by entrepreneurs. We could say – and this is ambivalence in the economic sphere in action: 'OK, you can have a private company worth up to a million pounds. After that, a degree of public or social ownership needs to be introduced.' In other words, the community must have a say after a certain wealth-point has been reached. Or we could make it illegal for entrepreneurs to borrow money privately from banks after their personal wealth and that of their company had reached a certain point. We could decide, by the usual processes of political debate, what that point would be.

The idea is to come to terms with our contradictory feelings about wealth rather than polarizing those feelings. We need to go beyond *either* wanting to stop budding entrepreneurs in their tracks *or* wanting them to go on and become Bill Gates or Rupert Murdoch. This psychological approach to economic policy involves placing some practical limitations on the growth of private companies and on the ways in which they are permitted to finance themselves. It would be a radical form of the 'stakeholding' proposed as a central economic idea by the Labour Party in Britain at the end of 1995 (see below for a further discussion of stakeholding).

But not everyone is going to be an entrepreneur. Could we create a psychological atmosphere in which we teach and encourage good-enough entrepreneurial skills but do not stigmatize or criticize entrepreneurial failures? 'Try to get rich, but if you don't make it, don't feel bad about it. Failure is inevitable.' At the moment the message is that business failure is a very serious business, almost a moral flaw.

In terms of the institutions required, we would need a plurality of economic institutions, ranging from private companies to large state corporations, with co-operatives (like the Mondragon co-operatives in the Basque country) somewhere in the middle. It would mean not committing ourselves to only one style of economic organization – a position that is difficult to sustain. There might continue to be a special role for pension funds or similar institutions, because these are in a sense already socialized or collective institutions. But their role would have to be statutorily modified under these proposals.

If we encouraged success but did not punish failure, we would have a more solid psychological background for legislation that made minimum wages at decent levels more likely. One reason so many Western countries do not have truly effective minimum-wage legislation is that they are enslaved to the idea of a clear success–failure divide. Well-paid 'failures' go against the grain. Exhorting success but not penalizing failure also leads to the consideration of ideas like social dividends or credits, which would replace social security and welfare systems.

Ultimately, if we allowed our ambivalence about wealth to flourish, we might end up with a substantial sector of the economy that was simply outside the business world altogether, that was not money-fuelled, or used money in the ordinary way: the exchange of services, perhaps by voucher or local currency systems, might become an alternative to the money system. The beginnings of such a development can be observed in several countries.

There are some wider things to consider here, such as the relatively new idea of the social audit. An audit measures the financial situation of a company. But a social audit measures things that have usually been regarded as non-measurable in financial terms. In a sense, a social audit is a psychological project. It tries to measure the ethical and even the emotional profit-and-loss situation of an organization by looking at what it is doing in relation to what it seeks to do, and above all at what it is doing in relation to what its 'stakeholders', who are not only shareholders but also employees, customers and the wider community, want it to do. Becoming psychological about economics means that certain inhibitions on thought get removed, and we can start to think in terms of measuring the unmeasurable, even conducting an 'emotional audit'.

It seems worth noting that even some corporations recognize the need for other than financial audits. When they are looking into acquiring another company, for example, the most progressive among them conduct not only a financial due diligence, which is an audit of the potential acquisition's 'hard' financial assets, but also a 'cultural due diligence', which evaluates how decisions get made, employees' ability to deal with change, the tolerance for mistakes within the organization, the willingness to take risks, and so on. Certain corporations also conduct an 'environmental due diligence', to make sure that the other company's operations and plants are reasonably clean and not likely to incur law suits or fines.

Some of these ideas have been floated before, especially by those on the left. What is perhaps novel in this psychologized version is that a conscious attempt is being made to get the benefit of both perspectives rather than resolving them into a spurious synthesis that will usually end up by favouring the modified marketeers, alloys being easier to work than gold. *The result looks contradictory because it is supposed to be contradictory*, drawing energy from the interplay and tension of competing viewpoints.[2] As Milton Friedman himself once said: 'The more significant the theory, the more unrealistic the assumptions.'

We need to consider how to extend the vocabulary of economics. If we use the metaphor of an iceberg where one-seventh is above the surface and six-sevenths below the surface, then most economic analysis seems to take place only in the top seventh. There are endless arguments about

how much it would cost to do this or that, or what the alternative benefits in terms of goods or services might be.

What if we began to think beyond 'exchange value' (cost
or price) to consider 'emotional value', 'aesthetic value' and
'sustainable value'? For example, what if developers or government departments favour road-building at the expense of
the environment? Could we argue that the emotional value
of preserving the environment will be greater than that of
the road or supermarket? Could we add that the development would also sacrifice aesthetic value? Is it valid to point
out that, if trees and natural habitats are destroyed, then
long-term sustainability is reduced?

We could also conduct an emotional audit of ourselves.
Living in a system characterized by extremes of inequality in
the distribution of wealth carries with it emotional costs for
all of us. Connections between physical health and wealth
have been extensively charted, as has the negative impact on
people's lives of unemployment, alienation in the workplace,
and changing patterns of employment. Less often discussed
are the psychological consequences of economic and social
injustice on those who apparently are reasonably well situated. To live in an unfair economic system has a psychologically debilitating effect on all of us, leading to widespread
anxiety about our general well-being. Economic instability
sets up a massively negative emotional field-effect that
reaches everyone.

WHAT DO YOU *REALLY* FEEL ABOUT ECONOMICS?

One psychological aspect of economics that has been explored in workshops concerns people's feelings about money

and inequalities of wealth.[3] If we really wanted to, we surely could do away with economic injustice. Hence, it becomes crucial to discover at depth why it is that we do *not* want to do away with it, why we embrace inequality. In these workshops, two themes often emerge. First, it is very difficult for well-meaning people to admit openly how much they *love* inequality of wealth. This discovery, and the creation of a safe space in which to confess to materialism, is in itself of psychological interest. But the second theme is of even greater interest. Alongside the love of money, the flaunting fantasies and the sadistic play – and often in the very same people – there is an equally powerful and active turning away from everything that is involved in espousing inequality of wealth. You often have to wade through fantasies of ostentation and exploitation of others to reach the equally secret disgust-driven commitment to a more fair economic system. But it is there, masked in part by our rules about having consistent views in areas of serious public concern like economics. For example, although it is easy to poke fun at people who are responsible for resource-greedy and polluting factories and then seek rural solace in a simpler life at weekends, the fact that so many middle-class people turn to the countryside and the great outdoors for some kind of refreshment perhaps shows that there is some energy available for the reduction of inequalities of wealth.

The meanings that any individual attributes to money are learned to a great extent within the family. Cash may be clung to or thrown away because of its perceived potential to make up for a sense of loss or to provide emotional warmth; to enhance personal worth, satisfy inchoate longings, or establish power over others. It is these emotional elements that explain some of the intensity of people's feelings about

153

money. Attitudes to money are also shaped by experiences of the wider world, and the interaction between social experience and personal history explains individual responses to such developments as increasing insecurity in employment or the crumbling of the welfare state.

Bringing psychology to economics enables us to see something very tangible in the economic world, something material, as suffused with emotion and fantasy. Hence the ironic section title 'What do you *really* feel about economics?'

Owning up to our complex feelings about wealth means owning up to our own criminality as well as our generosity. As the Moscow Mafia currently demonstrates, at the heart of market economics lies a form of economic criminality. (Proudhon's 'property is theft' expresses the notion succinctly.) But our economic criminality also links us to something that we tend to value rather highly: our ingenuity and gift for improvisation. The economic work of the Trickster shows itself in the burgeoning, informal 'parallel economies' of the world (such as the cocaine trade), without which many people would, quite simply, die of starvation. In Lima, one of every two people is sustained by the informal parallel economy. Let us think about this: on the one hand, criminality, unfairness, cheating, lying, stealing, death. On the other hand, ingenuity, energy, imagination, inspiration, improvisation, productivity, life. Psychological economics is not consistent; it requires us to relate to all these contradictory things in ourselves at the same time. We cannot just dispense with the problems of the psychology of theft because we want to enjoy the fruits of the psychology of economic ingenuity. As Balzac said, 'Every great fortune is founded upon a crime.'

In the workshops, the economic psyche is explored under four headings: economics past, economics present, economics benevolent, economics shameful.

Economics past: what was your first 'economic memory' – about money, or the economy, or your parents' jobs? What was the first time you became aware that there was an economic system in existence, with polarities of wealth and poverty, with inequities – the first memory of that kind? How was money dealt with in your family of origin? Who controlled it? What kind of source of difficulty, or ease, was it? What class did your family belong to, and how did family members feel about it?

Economics present: have you done better than your parents? If so, how do you feel about it? Have you done worse? If so, how do you feel about that? Have you done about the same? If so, how do you feel about it? How open about money are you, really? How do you handle money in your personal relationships?

Economics benevolent: how much more tax would you be prepared to pay if you knew and could control where it was going? What economic and material goodies could you do without?

Economics shameful: (I used to call this 'economics sadistic', but it put people off). Fantasize about the most shameful, sadistic, controlling, horrible thing you could or would do if you had a very large sum of money at your disposal – hundreds of millions of pounds, for example.

A professor of philosophy at one workshop in the United States said, 'Well, if I had unlimited funds, I'd buy thousands of acres of skiing land at Aspen and fence it off so nobody could use it.' I did not think that was very sadistic, to say the least. Then he added: 'And I'd hire the US Marine Corps to machine-gun anyone who came near.' He burst into tears and told us about his tycoon father and the relationship he had had with him and so on and so forth. So economics shameful does not involve just self-congratulatory fantasy about getting rid of capitalists. It is about owning our own bit of the system, a piece of shadow from which we can all too glibly detach ourselves.

PSYCHOTHERAPY AND ECONOMICS

A psychotherapeutic angle on economics appreciates from the outset that there will always be degrees of wastefulness and out-of-controlness in economic systems. Once human desire enters into any social system – as it always does – that system cannot function predictably. There are no final solutions to social questions. The social issues with which our societies are faced are as incorrigible, as unresponsive to treatment, as the psychological issues that individuals face. Just as we now know that there is no unified ego that stands in for the whole personality, there is no one unified economic citizen with a coherent agenda (and no unified version of society, either). That is what makes control of the social impossible. In today's consumption-oriented economies, understanding mass or collective psychology may offer some insight into the irrationality of the economic forces that we are subject to. But there are no universal social forms to fall back on, no essentialist economic archetypes that can solve all the problems for us. We have to start with minds as open as possible, paying free-floating, evenly hovering attention to economic matters.

Yet I wonder if the pessimistic tone of much contemporary psychoanalytic social criticism, especially in the Lacanian tradition, does not reflect a secret idealization of the fact that it is impossible to rectify the social dysfunctions we face. Psychoanalytic critics whose stress is on the permanent state of 'social rupture' that exists within a 'hegemonically structured society', and who are convinced that human subjectivity is 'contingent on a fundamental sense of lack', are not exactly going to be disappointed when constructive political intentions go awry or economic processes spiral out of control. Such an outcome only confirms their theories. They would argue that to expect anything different is infantile and grandiose. In the rush to be worldly wise and theoretically correct, some post-Lacanian psychoanalytic political theorists have lost sight of the fact that human beings are both made by *and* make the cultures in which they live. The psyche is both conservative *and* creative.[4]

But there is also real value in the kinds of psychoanalytic health warning being summarized. Painful though it is to accept, it serves to remind us that we may very well fail to make the changes we aspire to in a time frame that feels emotionally acceptable. In this way, psychoanalysis can provide us with a cold douche of realism.

We are still left with the unmistakable fact that the volatility of today's financial, futures and hedge markets resembles the psyche itself: their ups and downs, rapid swings of confidence and the huge emotional impact that non-economic events like the weather and sports results have on these markets. Just as there is nothing neutral in the system we call the psyche, so there is nothing neutral in the system we call the economy. The definite symbolic charge possessed by money can be elucidated, as we find in the workshops. It is deeply implicated in many exceedingly problematic fantasies. Anyone who still believes what the economics textbooks say about the neutrality of money and its consequent utility in processes of exchange is in denial!

The very etymology of the word 'money' has some fascinating implications for political and economic thought.[5] It stems from the Middle English word *monoie*, which comes from the Old French *monie*. That in turn stems from the Latin *moneta*, and both *moneta* and *monie* are feminine nouns. Moneta was also the name the Romans used for Mnemosyne, memory and the mother of the Muses. This comes from the verb *moneo* – I remind, put in mind, admonish, advise, warn, instruct, teach. The root of *moneo* is *men-*, which leads to other words like *memini* – I remember, recollect, think of, am mindful of. (Our word 'mention' comes from this root.) *Mens*, also coming from *men-*, can mean mind, heart, soul, but specifically refers to conscience, reason and rationality. Mens was the Roman goddess of thought, and there are also links to Minerva, the Roman Athena, goddess of wisdom, reflection, arts, sciences, poetry, weaving.

We see the outcroppings of these stems in words like monitor or mentor, and there are connections to admonition, prophecy and warning. The links that repay reflection are perhaps those to memory and conscience. The pervasiveness of these associations to 'money' shows that in modern economies all monetary and other transactions often have symbolic as well as actual connotations. Money is clearly more than psychoanalysis has sometimes made of it – 'deodorized, dehydrated shit that has been made to shine', in Ferenczi's words.

CHAPTER TEN

The political clinic

THIS CHAPTER reviews some explicit links between how psychotherapists work in practice and a new approach to the emotional dimensions of politics. Developing a psychological take on politics that encompasses feelings and sensibilities is not just an issue for the educated, chattering classes or for New Agers. Many people want to know how they can translate into effective and healing action their heartfelt emotional, imaginative and bodily responses to political scenarios such as Kosovo, ecological disaster, homelessness and poverty. How can they begin to make political use of their private reactions to public events? Could citizens model themselves on psychotherapists so as to become therapists of the world, *citizens-as-therapists*? If so, they will need to make use of their 'countertransference', a term that may require a brief explanation.

A NOTE ON COUNTERTRANSFERENCE

People who have never been analysts or therapists are often surprised to learn that clinical practice is a red-hot emotional activity. It is not usually the case that a client quietly reports a problem to a therapist who then explains its origins by reference to specialized knowledge about such matters as childhood trauma or the significance of chains of association. Instead, the therapist's state of mind in relation to the client often shows signs of altered levels of consciousness. The presence of intense fantasy and aroused emotion may lead to disturbed bodily and behavioural functioning. It is these central features of the therapist's experience, which are the regular currency of discussion among clinicians, that have been tagged as the 'countertransference'.[1]

Hence it is possible for therapists to review their experience (anything but calm) in a calm and professional way, underscoring its utility and resisting the tendency to conclude that they are simply prone to mad responses to their clients. Although no hard-and-fast methodological consensus exists about the *use* of the countertransference, a definite historical trend in theorizing about it can be observed. In this trend, countertransference experiences of the therapist are understood as communications from the client to the therapist and hence as having clinical utility.

In a research project into countertransference that I conducted, therapists and analysts reported the following wide range of countertransference experiences:

❖ First, *bodily and behavioural responses.* For example, wearing the same clothes as the client, walking into a lamp-post, forgetting to discuss something important, a strange sensation in the solar plexus, a pain in a particular part of the body, sexual arousal, sleep.

❖ Second, *feeling responses.* For example: anger, impatience, a sense of power, a sense of powerlessness, envy, irritation, depression, boredom.

❖ Finally, *fantasy responses.* For example: this is the wrong client, there's something wrong with my feet, a large black pot, I killed her mother, I'm a prostitute, I feel reverence for her serious, private place, *he* has God on *his* side, all colour has gone out of the world, a car crash, he'll rummage through my desk and books if I leave the room, the client is getting bigger and bigger and is filling the room.[2]

All the respondents in the research project indicated that they regarded countertransference experiences like these as usable communications from the client. They did not rule out overlap with neurotic areas in themselves, but they made it clear – and this is typical of contemporary clinical practice – that they could live with that possibility in order to make full use of what they were 'picking up' from their clients.

THE POLITICAL CLINIC

To return to politics, closing the gap between subjective and emotional experiences of politics on the one hand and public policy on the other is a key background political issue of our times. Mainstream politicians do not pay enough attention to it. Perhaps this is because of deep uncertainty about how to translate passionately held political convictions from emotional states into something that actually works on the ground.

Over the past few years, I have been running workshops and conferences on psychological approaches to politics in several countries. This work testifies to the fact that people are much more 'political' than they think they are. They know far more about the political events of the day than they think they do – though this knowledge does not always take the official forms of a grasp of statistics or history. Gradually, participants discover that, all their lives, they have been far better informed about the political world than they thought they were. It has been fascinating hearing about people's first memories of political events, their first recognition that there is something one could call a political system, the first time they had to face up to the fact that there are many competing ideas about how to run that system. On numerous occasions, relating their first political memory (not necessarily the strongest one they can think of) has reduced participants to tears; it has proven traumatic and/or cathartic. (Virtually none of the participants who have had psychotherapy have ever discussed the memory in therapy.)

Similarly, what also becomes clear is that people have more and stronger political commitments than they knew about – a kind of 'repression' has been in operation. These commitments need time to emerge from within and do not always quickly take the outer form of signing petitions, going on demonstrations, or voting. Such hidden, buried, silent sources of political wisdom stem from the private, secret 'countertransference' reactions everyone has to what is going on in the political world. Yet such private reactions have no ready outlet, since they are all too often dismissed as 'subjective'.

For example, at a political clinic in New York, shortly after the Los Angeles riots of April 1992, a largely non-professional audience was asked to bring to the surface and record their emotional, fantasy, dream and physical responses to the riots. Doing this in a contained setting had a very powerful effect. The participants said that they had often reacted in a bodily or other highly personal way to numerous political events, as well as the riots. But they feared these secret responses would not pass muster in everyday political discourse. Their conception of official politics fitted in with the definition of what our leaders would like us to accept – as a purely objective activity.

When we came to discuss the riots in a more rational vein, the audience came up with a range of novel, imaginative and practical ideas about urban and ethnic problems. They felt that 'the political' was redefined, reframed, revisioned. Most of those present did not believe that there were avenues available in official political culture for what often gets stigmatized as an irrational approach. Their assessment is right. Using a perspective derived from one hundred years of the practice of therapy, in which so-called irrational responses *are* honoured and heeded, is a small step towards creating a new, more psychological approach to the problems of power and politics.

At another political clinic in Santa Barbara, California, the group chose to work with the theme of homelessness in the United States. That is, as citizens-as-therapists, they were confronted with a client called 'Homelessness in America'. The audience on this occasion contained several people with backgrounds and experience in housing and related social policy areas (though no one was actually homeless). One thing that emerged is how rarely we feel 'at home'; homelessness is, in a way, the more 'normal' state. Yet in industrial cultures, the fixed and stable home is always regarded as 'where we start from', in T. S. Eliot's words.

The process of the workshop destabilized this assumption as the participants renormalized homelessness. But homelessness is an awful state to be in and, very often, something practical needs to be done about it. As far as policy went, it was felt to be essential to provide for periods of homelessness by, for example, making it easier rather than more difficult to drop out of emergency accommodation or housing programmes. Moreover, swapping arrangements would be needed allowing nomadic citizens to use temporary shelters geographically distant from programmes with which they were registered. (Such arrangements do not presently exist, we were told.) Other practical proposals included free depositories for possessions and some kind of ride-sharing scheme. These proposals came out of discussions that followed the segment of the workshop in which the far less rational 'countertransferences' were expressed. Their down-to-earthness acknowledged the fact that saying homelessness is a state of mind (alienation) is very different from not having a roof over your head.

At a political clinic on racism in Britain, at which several specialists in race relations were present, we started to get countertransference images of pristine environments, such as mountain tops, beaches, lakes – all places where there were not only no Black people, but no people at all. Reflecting on this collection of similar subjective responses to racism as a 'client', the group became conscious of something more profoundly anti-human in racism than they had been aware of before. Most of the group had previously adhered to the standard psychodynamic explanation for racism: you put your bad bits, the bits you would like to eliminate, into another person or group, thereby cleaning yourself up and making yourself feel superior. But we found that, at some level, racists actually want to eliminate themselves.

Experiences in political clinics like these led me to start speaking of citizens-as-therapists. It is clear that things usually regarded as exceptionally private – early experiences in the family, dreams, fantasies, bodily sensations – may be understood in a different way and turned into useful and even transformative political tools.

In the workshop, the group chooses the political theme on which they want to focus. They are asked to imagine themselves as therapists and the political theme as the client. They relax, maybe lie down, and pay attention to their breathing. One person acts as a scribe. The participants say whatever comes into their minds in relation to the political theme, whether it is thoughtful, playful or fantastical, and also do their best to concentrate on and verbalize any bodily reactions they are having in response to the political theme. They should not censor anything but say whatever it is that comes up *regardless of its irreverence, irrelevance or lack of political correctness*. The scribe tries to write everything down. Then the results are scanned, and anything that is obviously rational (no matter how seemingly right) gets discarded. What remains may or may not fall into strands of imagery or ideas. Either way, the group discusses what is there and sees if there is a pattern. When they have done this, they proceed to have an 'ordinary' discussion on the political theme they have chosen, but with a greater capacity to deal with the problem than they might have had before participating in this exercise. When the membership of the workshop includes those who have no experience or knowledge of therapy, a brief explanation of 'countertransference' is given.

Notions of citizenship have changed quite dramatically over historical time. That term 'the politician within' may be regarded as a contribution to the evolving history of citizenship. The idea that citizens can (and do) approach the problems of the world in which they live as if they were its therapists and it was their client constitutes a radical shift in what we expect or imagine a citizen to be. One could say, 'I am going to do my politics like an architect, acknowledging the need for foundations.' Or, 'I am going to do my politics like an artist, seeking the image or phrase that opens up the door to a larger perspective.' Why should one not try to do politics like a therapist? In such a case, the citizen-as-therapist approaches politics in the same ethos of unknowing and humility that characterizes all good clinical work.

This is a difficult idea to accept because it rests on the novel notion that political problems want to communicate with us, their potential therapists. The problems are talking to us, the street is talking to us, the housing crisis, the problem of unemployment, civil strife – all are talking to us. Like any therapist and client, both sides of the relationship – citizen and political problem – inhabit the same world. Instead of regarding the citizen as a client, which is what often happens when therapists discuss politics, we make the scene-shifting step of regarding the citizen as the therapist.

Recasting the citizen as a therapist means that the citizen is entitled to use whatever it is that therapists make use of in working with their clients. When we consider people's spontaneous reactions to politicians, political events or just the nature of the political in modern societies, we have seen that there is a kind of tacit, private, secret political intelligence and wisdom at work. Locked up in people's narratives of their experiences in the world is a critique of that world. The point is greatly expanded when we recall that we are all the time having images and experiences of the world that we do not even know we are having; these take us ever deeper into the political psyche.

This more psychological way of speaking the political

favours participation by those who are presently on the margins of power: women, gay men and lesbians, members of ethnic minorities, those in transgressive families, the physically challenged, the economically disadvantaged, psychiatric patients; these are the people whose subjective responses to politics constitute their resources. Those diverse groupings should not be regarded as Marx did his hopeless lumpenproletariat. Rather, they are the last untapped founts of new energies and ideas in the political and social realms. Disempowered people certainly need the kind of economic and financial transfusions that only politics of the official kind can presently offer. But they might also derive a form of political power by making use of the feelings, fantasies, behaviours and embodiments that are banned and marginalized in the late-modern world. There is a potential in everyone to be a therapist of the world. Throughout our lives, all of us have had private responses to politics. We need to raise to the level of cultural consciousness the kind of politics that people have secretly carried within themselves. Citizens, informed by and armed with therapy's own power to make something useful out of subjectivity, can take their place as citizens-as-therapists.

Analysts and therapists already have texts that teach them how to translate their impressions, intuitions, gut responses, bodily reactions, fantasies and dreams about clients into hard-nosed professional treatment approaches. They already have the idea that their subjective responses are precious, valid, relevant, effective – and there is some knowledge about how to act on those responses. So, without realizing it perhaps, therapists and clients have something that could be shared with the disempowered or with political thinkers and activists who have nothing to do with the practice of psychotherapy. After all, just as client and therapist are in it together, so, too, do citizen and political problem inhabit – quite literally – the same space.

All citizens – not just those involved in therapy – could start to function as therapists of the political world, learning to use their bodily and other subjective reactions as organs of political wisdom, helping themselves to understand the problems of the political more deeply and guiding the course of their actions. The evolution of a kind of political knowledge analogous to the therapeutic encounter would also reflect the fact that many people already possess a therapeutic attitude to the world. Many want to participate in nothing less than the resacralization of our culture by becoming therapists of the world. We all know that, as citizens, we have bodily and other subjective reactions to the political. But it rarely occurs to us that the political, with its problems, its pain, its one-sidedness, may actually be trying to communicate with us, its therapists. Does politics truly want therapy? Could we encourage it to come to its first session?

This 'therapeutic' way of speaking and doing politics may at first sound like an over-personal, hysterical approach. But it could be one path left open to us in our flattened, over-controlled, cruel and dying political world. What official politics rejects as shadow – and what can undoubtedly still function as shadow – may just turn out to have the ultimate level of value, which is a typical pattern of discovery in therapy.

In the world of the consulting room, as we have seen, the move is from the therapist's subjectivity to an understanding of the client's psychic reality; in the world of politics, the move is from the citizen's subjectivity to an understanding of the culture's social reality. We can take a sentence from a clinical text like this one of Christopher Bollas's and rewrite it in more political terms: 'It is essential to find some way to put forward for analytic investigation that which is occurring in the analyst as a purely subjective and private experience.'[3] It becomes: 'It is essential to find some way to put forward for *political* investigation that which is occurring in the *citizen* as a purely subjective and private experience.'

Several art and literary critics have referred explicitly to providing therapy for an art work or text.[4] Some historians also seem to regard themselves as offering therapy to their topics of interest.[5] And the imagery of psychotherapy already permeates the environmental movement (ecopsychology). So it has been recognized that it is not absolutely necessary to have a client in human form in order to do therapy work.

THE BODY IN POLITICS

In clinical therapy, the therapist's bodily reactions are a highly important pathway to the client's psychic reality. Similarly, the political therapist's bodily reactions are an important part of the picture: the body is an organ of information. Bodily reactions to the surface of modern life, its sounds, smells, textures and shapes; bodily reactions to the demands of modern life, its crush, bustle, hassle and artery-blocking stresses. Bodily reactions, worked on and distilled in ways familiar to the clinical therapist, lead the political therapist to the heart of the culture and its political problems. The body of the political therapist leads in a spontaneous political therapy. Affect, bodily sensations, wild fantasies, are all reframed and re-evaluated as the tools of political analysis. In existing political discourse, there is no psychologically valid account of how we can take fear, disgust, a sense of contamination, anger and all the rest of the somatic lexicon as indicators of our political judgements.

Though a body-based analysis of political themes and problems will take place spontaneously, it is nevertheless possible to sketch out three stages or rather levels of a somatic analysis of the political. First, we need to undertake a thorough exploration of the bodily state, both the body as a whole and its constituent parts. This requires practice and training and an atmosphere and setting that are friendly to the enterprise. Second, we have to learn the particular language of the body when it engages in political discourse. We need to focus, clarify, differentiate and describe the somatic vocabulary and the bodily imagery involved. Third, we have to make explicit the implicit meanings of such imagery in an act of interpretation.[6]

SUBJECTIVE POLITICS

Up to now, having empathy with a political problem has been seen from the standpoint of conventional politics as having an 'emotional' reaction to the problem (and nothing kind is meant by the word emotional in this context). Being emotional about politics is too often seen as being biased, unreliable, 'unsound'; it is sometimes seen, also, as implying a 'feminine' attitude to politics (and nothing kind is meant by feminine here, either).

The 'masculine' cast of so-called objective political analysis may have its roots in the psychological need of children to move away from a dependent relationship with either mother or father or both. To help themselves achieve personal boundaries – a clear sense of personal identity – some individuals tip over into a rather rigid attitude to the world, with an accent on distance and precision. This comes through as political 'objectivity' and is experienced as incontrovertibly objective even when its objectivity is exposed by others as a disguised subjectivity. The feeling of being politically objective imparts a bleak political strength. But those who continue to maintain their political objectivity are often uncomfortable with feeling deeply *involved* in social and political problematics. Perhaps they fear, unconsciously, that muddled feelings will inevitably lead to a return to the parental corral. So politics can be approached only from outside, as it were, because staying outside avoids a merger with the parent/political problematic – a merger that is experienced as identity-threatening.

A question is bound to be raised concerning subjective politics. Has it not led to undesirable mass hysterias, such as Nazism or racism, or to markedly populist leaders such as Mrs Thatcher? And you want *more* of this? As far as mass movements go, the diametrically opposite argument can be made: they destroy rather than foster the space for subjectivity in politics, in that mass movements are hostile to whatever is unique to an individual subject and his or her psychological functioning.

If one tries to see populist leaders as therapists of the world, then they resemble those guru-like therapists who approach their clients with pre-existing assumptions about what constitutes well-being and how to achieve it. Populist leaders like Mrs Thatcher are generally not *responding* to the citizen; they are usually *imposing* something upon the citizen out of their own systems of belief. Just as guru-therapists often get good results in the very short term, so, too, populist leaders seem to offer quick solutions to political problems. But, in both instances, before very long the complexity and incorrigibility of psychological or political problems defeats these magical cures.

CONCLUDING REFLECTIONS

The language, values and, above all, the practices of psychotherapy contribute towards a politics that manages the irrational creatively. In so doing, psychotherapy remains true to its own roots and its knowledge that there are differing modes of consciousness. But, as Russell Jacoby points out, the actual potential of psychotherapy itself to frighten the institutions of an oppressive society has leached away: 'Over the years the ghost has become a ghost of itself'.[7] The apparently inflated fancy of providing therapy for the world does not rest on models of the psyche or theories of child development. It is clinical method, used wildly out of context, that turns out to have something to offer.

We will end by completely reversing the poles of the chapter in a way that will seem threatening to therapy and therapists. Up to now, we have seen how the clinical approach of countertransference can be turned to political use. But perhaps there is also a 'political' explanation for the countertransferences that therapists experience, that makes unconscious-to-unconscious communication possible. In this reading of it, there could be no communication between therapist and client without there being social and political linkages between them. Their joint citizenship and joint occupation of the same political and social spaces are powerful connecting links. Literally, they are in the same state. If countertransference is an essential ingredient of therapy, and if it is possible only because of the political factor, then the way we have been counterposing 'therapy' and 'politics', with the former contributing to the latter, needs balancing. Neither is superior to or more fundamental than the other.

CHAPTER ELEVEN

Psychotherapy, the citizen and the state

T RADITIONALLY, ONE defines a social entity, such as a state, by looking for its core values and practices, around which a consensus has developed. But this is old-fashioned thinking. We need instead to start our field-defining work at the outer limits of the envelope. And what actually defines a state, from a psychological perspective, is dispute within it.

How does this work in practice? If citizens are having an argument about a political topic, and you have some idea what they are talking about, and you are in some way psychologically stirred by their argument, then you are part of the same state. That is, one way to define a state is by the emotional ripples such arguments generate. In this pluralistic reading of political culture, we stay with the debates, disagreements, miscommunications, misunderstandings, betrayals and onslaughts on one another, rather than with the core, the centre, the consensus, harmony. A. N. Whitehead expressed this idea beautifully when he said: 'A clash of doctrines is not a disaster, it is an opportunity.'

Pluralism is an attitude to conflict that tries to reconcile differences without imposing a false resolution on them or losing sight of the unique value of each position. It is not the same as multiplicity (or, in social and political terms, multiculturalism). Rather, it attempts to hold unity and diversity in balance – humanity's age-old struggle in politics, religion and philosophy to honour the tension between the One (for example, a modern, unified, melting-pot state) and the Many (for example, multicultural, identity-based politics in the contemporary fashion). The trademark of pluralism is competition and its way of life is bargaining. The tensions between the world-views of the One and the Many exist for us because we are directly affected by both perspectives. Many features of contemporary culture thrust us in the direction of global oneness: space exploration (which first offered us an image of the planet as a whole), telecommunications and television leading to the creation of a global village, Hollywood and other manifestations of American culture, and the rise of multinational corporations and economic globalization. But there is manyness in our world as well: civic, ethnic and generational strife, collapse of national boundaries and a series of forced migrations (the twentieth century has been called the 'refugee century') – and, on the more positive side, we are invited to celebrate diversity, accept intermarriage and, in the wake of Einstein, face the challenges of relativity on all levels – cultural as well as in terms of physics.

On a personal level, citizens are faced with the pluralistic task of aligning many internal voices and self-images with the wish and need to speak with one voice and recognize themselves as an integrated being, a unified citizen. This is an issue of intense feeling; the politician within, introduced in Chapter 2, is not likely to live harmoniously with himself or herself.

Next, a pluralistic approach may be of help in dealing with issues of social unity and diversity as they crop up in contemporary politics. For example, political philosophers refer to an 'identity/difference' theme, meaning that, in some ways, each citizen is identical (we are all One) and, in other ways, each citizen is different (we are Many). If both are true, then what is needed is an ethos, which would have to be drawn equally from psychology and from politics, to underpin the identity/difference theme.

The fragmentation and dispute within a state, as each group fights for the general acceptance of its viewpoint, seems, on the surface, to be the very opposite of what is usually regarded as pluralism. However, aggressive competitiveness can be understood as lying at the heart of a pluralistic approach to politics. Ideas such as those of unconscious compensation (Jung) and reaction formation (Freud) suggest that we should look a little more deeply into the warlike situations that pertain in so many situations. What do they compensate (that is make up for, balance) in the collective psyche? What less aggressive fantasies and impulses are they reactive to? Can we read and interpret divisive surface phenomena in other ways? Aggression, which is so prevalent in modern societies, often masks the deepest need for contact, dialogue, playback, affirmation.

From this interpretative perspective, what seems like a political flight from pluralism may also be regarded as an unconscious longing for whatever pluralism might imply – tolerance, compassion, vigorous yet respectful argument between competing individuals and interest groups. As Heraclitus put it, 'that which alone is wise both wishes and does not wish to be called Zeus.'

There are good reasons why such a longing exists in contemporary states, for a pluralistic attitude balances the tension between the claims of and tendencies towards a unified society and the claims of and tendencies towards diversity in society. It would not be pluralistic, as the word is used here, merely to assert that there are many diverse truths about politics and to leave it there, with pluralism simply equalling multiculturalism. Rather, truth with a small t (here, cultural diversity) has to compete with Truth with a big T (here, the unified, homogeneous state). Sometimes, passionate and even aggressive expressions of and adherence to the Truth could (even should) be the right way to live. But sometimes we need a more partial and pragmatic vision of multiple truths, equally passionate and aggressive in its own way.

Many citizens are probably committed in their own minds to dialogue, to straddling the divide between Truth and truth, but the psychological difficulties associated with maintaining a tolerant attitude cannot be minimized. Citizens, being human, will continually fail to be as tolerant as they would like to be. In part, this is because of their devotion to their own approaches to politics which, after all, carry what they consider they need for survival and a good life. Citizens are bound to be passionately committed to their own particular visions or personal confessions of politics.

But where is any kind of programme to combine tolerance with passion in society? We know about the opposites of tolerance very well – extremism, envy, denigration, control, fundamentalism, authoritarianism and so forth. But, understandably, we usually pathologize these, whether politically or psychologically. My intention is to do something positive with the incorrigible competitiveness and argumentativeness within society, mining it for the tension-rich gold it might contain. Competition that is open, competition that is brought into consciousness, competition that is psychologically integrated and valued, could lead to a tough-minded tolerance. The idea is to stay close to and trade off the energy of what Jung called the shadow – the thing each of us has no wish to be. To paraphrase Lacan, if the human unconscious is structured like anything, it may be structured like a political argument.

Through argument and competition with other citizens, we come to know ourselves and our ideas better and more deeply. In many psychological theories, there is an important mirroring Other, in relation to whom psychological life takes place.[1] This Other is a creative entity and needs nurturing. In politics, the Other is officially the opponent and usually experienced as an obstacle to be removed. But the opposing Other will not go away no matter how ardently you wish he or she would. The Other is omnipresent and indestructible. Sure, you can describe your opponent in unflattering terms and do horrible things to your opponent. But, in one form or another, the opponent will bounce back, rejecting the distortions, resisting your manoeuvres, and returning to the argument. That is why we may expect to see a rejuvenated Opposition of some kind in Britain during the first decade of the twenty-first century. Confrontation and dialogue go on in societies even when it seems they have been stilled (as the great political changes in Europe and South Africa in the 1990s showed us).

Amidst the seemingly ridiculous political infighting and name-calling of conventional politics, a kind of exchange is constantly being crafted. When we project something on to another person or group, it is often the good or positive things about ourselves that are projected. On the individual level, re-collection of projected contents is vital for the health and integrity of the self. With these thoughts in mind, I suggest that we are all secret pluralists, but that the prevailing ideologies in most societies force us to deny this on the surface.

Let us see how the anxiety-provoking contemporary question of the extent to which states can function multiculturally responds to a pluralistic treatment. Some citizens tend to prefer, see and search for multiplicity and differentiation in society. Often, they belong to minority communities and the need to maintain the (ethnic, sexual, generational) identity of their own minority community feels paramount. Other citizens, coming or claiming to come from the majority, will be more inclined to favour integration and unity in society. From a pluralistic point of view, each position is denuded without the incorporation of elements of its opposite. To be a full citizen, to enjoy the benefits of a meeting with the politician within, it is not advisable to espouse only one of the two positions. But it is very hard to establish social and political conditions under which citizens with widely differing viewpoints can take note of each other, without having synthesis as a goal. A modular, conversational approach to politics in which different world views meet but do not try to take each other over is vulnerable to the knee-jerk adversarialism of much contemporary politics and to the media which treats political dispute in terms of winners and losers.

When ideas about policy are in competition, what attitudes to the competition are open to citizens? We can deny doubt and simply choose between policies and viewpoints – but that can lead to blind partisanship and possibly to tyranny. We can synthesize policies and viewpoints – but the resultant 'third way' may lead to an avoidance of the hard edges of disagreement rather than to a transcendence of them; no policy at all. Of course, we can take up an attitude of indifference to political dispute, as very many citizens do today, but that leads to ennui, collective depression and a subtle form of omnipotent fantasy in which the relevance of political debate and of politics itself is denied; politics gets replaced by shopping or meditation.

THE STATE AS A PART OF THE STATE

Over the years, I have observed how many of the vicissitudes of the psychotherapy world can be imaginatively conceived of as microcosmic of the larger political world – psychotherapy as a metaphor for society.

Within psychotherapy in Britain, and in other countries, there has been much intense discussion about the role (and worth) of national umbrella organizations that incorporate all the various modalities and distinctive schools of psychotherapy. The umbrella organizations cover the profession as a whole, and their central committees have powers over all aspects of the organization and work of the various component training bodies. The umbrella organization (standing in here, metaphorically, for the state) is not only a container and a regulator of everything going on within it. To the contrary, the umbrella organization is itself a special interest group. Supposedly the container of the whole, it is also a part of the whole. Paradoxically, what looks like the big thing is only in certain respects and at certain moments the big thing. At other times and in other respects, what looks like the big thing is only one of a number of littler things.

Thinking on the metaphorical level about psychotherapy umbrella organizations shows how wedded we are to either maternal or paternal models for political organizations and the state itself. In the maternal model, the big thing, the umbrella organization, 'holds' everything in it, just as Winnicott as mother holding baby. In the paternal model, the umbrella organization sets standards and guidelines and intervenes in 'criminal' situations when the regulations have been broken. A pluralistic model of (professional) politics tries to move beyond family tropes altogether to find a new approach to the relations between the umbrella organization as a whole and the rest. By the simple yet complex device of reconceiving the whole as a part of the whole, we can make a psychologically valid beginning at working out a new model for the relations of citizens and the state.

Many people see the state as the container of everything in a society, or at least of everything 'political' within a society. But we have seen that a state may also be regarded as a special interest group within society. If the state has as its goal the construction of a unified (that is not multicultural) society, then this may be regarded as the goal, not only of the whole state, but also, via the paradox mentioned just now, of a part of the state. Political process in a single society consists of arguments, competitions and bargaining between the diverse interest groups, and perhaps the state has a special regulatory role here. But its regulatory role also constitutes a special interest on behalf of itself. When we are talking about regulation, the state may well be special. But when we are talking about other things – art, education, trade, community relations – it does not necessarily have a special role.

What we usually think of as the unifying factor, the container, the core, the regulator, the circumference is also one of the parts. To take the analogy back to psychology, the ego has often been regarded as fulfilling the functions of 'the state' for an individual. But, as many analysts have pointed out, the ego is nothing more than one part of the psyche competing with other parts. In modern societies, the state has to argue for its place in the sun.

DIVERSITY IN POLITICS

Although pluralism may not equate with multiplicity or diversity, such ideas are closely linked to it. Hence, I want to ask if diversity can be analysed so as to reveal its special requirements and guidelines? And can we develop a vision of cultural diversity which simultaneously makes a place for political unity? For we should recall that pluralism does not simply mean diversity or multiplicity, not just the Many.

Freedom does not guarantee diversity, for freedom can lead to a part of a system expanding to wield a tyrannical hold over the whole. If I am free to do or be what I like, this can produce an unequal state of affairs between you and me. To make sure that does not happen, we may be required by political consensus or law to be more equal in some or all respects. But then an inhibition has been placed on my freedom. This is the conundrum that faces the citizen today. If I act on, live out, hold dear, fight for my ideas and my identity, what am I to do with the differing points of view and ways of life of which I am aware? I cannot just deny that they exist. My freedom to have a particular point of view may lead to an unhelpful, destructive denigration and abandonment of other people's ideas to the ultimate detriment of my own position and personal psychological well-being.

Equality does not guarantee diversity either. Instead, it may give rise to a bland, mediocre, passionless tolerance that leads to widespread indifference and boredom. This can be seen in the attitude some modern politicians have towards ideological differences: they do not matter when compared to practical inevitabilities. Such myopic, pragmatic triumphalism overlooks the fact that everything in a society is suffused with ideology and theory. If all views are considered to be of equal worth, what is to become of the freedom to feel a special value attaching to one's own view?

So neither the freedom to think and act nor an egalitarian approach to thought and action can be said to guarantee cultural diversity in a way that permits a unified view of society to coexist with it. But in case the problem lies with the way I have formulated things, maybe, rather than just advancing pluralism as a desirable state or goal, we should begin instead to *use* it as a *tool* or *instrument*. The purpose is to monitor the political mosaic, making sure that political diversity does not lead to destructive schism and that differences between particular points of view are not dishonestly smoothed over.

Political dispute and struggle give life to a society. They also serve to define the society generally and act as an access route for those who want to participate in politics. It is not only important that we see people in dispute as right or wrong, though it is vital to have views about that. We also have to consider whether they know what the other side is talking about. It is really rather hard to be completely wrong in politics. As Kafka put it, 'the correct perception of a matter and a complete misunderstanding of the matter do not totally exclude one another.'

So, instead of searching for one guiding political theory or abandoning theory altogether, we should consider several competing theories together and organize our civic life around such competition. What holds the diversity of politics together is that society holds together just as for disputatious modern sub-atomic physicists, their subject, the universe, holds together. Passion for one approach is complemented by passion for a plurality of approaches.

PROBLEMS OF PLURALISM

Let us consider now some of the problems a citizen faces when confronted with political pluralism of this kind. For all manner of psychological reasons, it is very hard to get worked up about being tolerant, to be a radical centrist, to go in for what Walter Bagheot called 'animated moderation'. Does pluralism condemn us to lose the excitement of breakthrough ideas, which are more likely to be held with passionate conviction? Or does such a worry rest on a misunderstanding and an idealization of the cycle of creativity? So-called 'new' ideas emerge from a pluralistic matrix and are re-absorbed into such a matrix. As Winnicott put it paraphrasing T. S. Eliot: 'It is not possible to be original except on the basis of a tradition.'[2] Ideas do not come into being outside of a context, nor does the new necessarily destroy the old; it often coexists with it. So what looks like inspirational political conviction arises from a plural *mise-en-scène* though it is convenient not to acknowledge the debt. And before we facilely hail the man or woman of vision, let us not forget Yeats's words: 'the worst are full of passionate intensity.' The well-known political benefits of having conviction in one's ideas can still be available, but can coexist with open communication and the chance to learn from diversity.

Passion can abide in dialogue and tolerance as much as it does in monologue and fanaticism. The citizen has never been able to live in isolation from others in the same society who have a different viewpoint. People have to fight with one another because they cannot ignore one another. Leaving aside the never to be settled question of whether any one political approach is more 'successful' than others, the arrogance of isolation was never a viable option.

CHAPTER TWELVE

Exploring national psychologies

E VERYONE 'KNOWS' that the nations of the world have different psychological characteristics and hence that individual members of these nations will display typical characteristics. We all have our favourite lists. Jokes and anecdotes depending on this 'knowledge' abound. More seriously, wars have been fought on the basis of it. Would it be helpful to clarify to what extent national psychologies genuinely differ, due to history and experience, cultural process and institutional dynamics, rather than some kind of national hard-wiring? Could this be done in ways other than the statistical and the economistic work currently being undertaken? Maybe, in a small way, a project of this kind would increase mutual understanding between nations. This will be important as we move into the new century with the possibility or even likelihood of renewed conflict between nations on everyone's mind.

Liberal suspicions of the seductive but negative appeal of nationalism have, quite understandably, delayed serious attempts to explore whether or not separate nations actually display identifiable and intelligible psychological characteristics. Psychological insight certainly needs to be brought to bear on the phenomenon of nationalism itself: how it works psychologically, what it does for people in both in-groups and out-groups, why it has so often been deployed in illiberal projects up to and including ethnic cleansing and death camps. Yet such inquiry has not gone very deeply into the question of different national psychologies. As the Dutch historian G. J. Renier put it:

> Outside men's minds there can be no nationality, because nationality is a way of looking at oneself, not an entity *an sich*. Common sense is able to detect it, and the only discipline that can describe and analyse it is psychological.[1]

During the twentieth century, everyone had reason to fear the excesses of violence and inhumanity stimulated by nationalism – even though social historians have pointed out the democratizing influence of nationalism as peoples honoured and developed their own particular cultures outside of transnational empires or papal authority. For many people, just to be able to read their national poets in their national language at long last has been no small triumph. It might be worth exploring whether the historic benevolence and communality of nationalism could be rediscovered.

The answers to psychological questions about nationalism will be (and have been) rather predictable and, in a certain sense, somewhat circular and reductive. It is a good example of the way the insights of psychology tend to be imposed on the social and historical processes under examination – a sort of triumphant 'psychological' nationalism. So psychological theorists whose main preoccupation is with the father and his desire to 'castrate' the opposition might tend to apprehend nationalism in terms of leaders – authoritarian, even Fascist figures like Hitler – and led – the swooning, submissive masses who followed him. Other theorists, more concerned with intrapsychic processes and mechanisms, will tell us about the crucial role of projection (of unwanted characteristics and features) on to internal minorities and external enemies: Jews are defilers of the Aryan race; Slavs are sub-humans; the French are by nature traitorous and dishonourable. By vanquishing them, the emergent nation is cleansed and purified.

Such attempts to understand the psychology of nationalism tell us as much about psychology as about nationalism. A much more interesting yet delicate project is the attempt to see if the claim most nationalisms have to make – that our nation is psychologically different from all other nations – is correct or not. If psychology has any role to play in understanding and helping to solve conflicts between nations (or internal conflicts of a nationalistic cast within nations), then we need to know something about national peculiarities in action. Just as a marital therapist needs to understand something about the warring partners even if the focus is on the whole system of the marriage, so the psychological specialist in national conflicts needs similar information about the protagonists with whom he or she is engaged.

Continuing to develop the analogy with therapy, though, as ever, conscious of its limitations, inquirers into the psychology of a particular nation both can and cannot effectively manage their own prejudices, emotions and subjective responses to that nation. For example, if I am considering whether or not there is an identifiable Israeli national psychology, I must acknowledge that, in so doing, I am approaching the issue both as a Jew and as a Briton. I can attempt to preserve my 'academic' neutrality or, in accord with contemporary therapy practice, openly admit these features of my response and try to make good use of them. What I cannot do is to pretend that such a response does not exist.

The difficulty is that there is no still point; everyone has a perspective, personal experiences and a history of their own. Everyone is coming from somewhere. In academic circles, the problem most often cited in this context is that of 'Eurocentrism', and it is certainly true that in the West 'we' hear more about how 'we' see 'them' than about how 'they' see 'us'. Other dangers range from methodological carelessness to an unwitting encouragement of fantasies of superiority and excellence. If we find that Moabites are particularly proud and aggressive, how can we stop this from being regarded as either the be-all and end-all of national existence or, conversely, the worst possible thing a nation can be?

What follows is a sort of checklist of principles that might protect an inquiry into the validity of the idea that different nations do have distinct psychological characteristics of their own from these dangers.

When considering individual citizens, we might recall that nationality is not the only factor at work in the formation of their social identity. As we have observed throughout this book, citizens are plural people. Their economic position, religious background, family history, age, sex, sexual orientation and so on exist in dynamic interplay with their national origin. Now, it may be possible to collect evidence about how such political variables (economics, sex, age, etc.) play themselves out in different national cultures. Can we find categories or 'boxes' which, while maybe not universal, are sufficiently ubiquitous to be discernible as discrete experiential entities? The monolith of nationalism can be broken up, at least on the level of individual experience.

Hence, the idea would be to take, say, 'sex', meaning the experience of being male or female and, so to speak, collect information about that experience within different national locations. So the question would not be 'What is Japan like?' nor even 'What are the Japanese like?' but 'What has been the experience of a Japanese man?' and then 'What has been the experience of a working-class Japanese man?' and then 'What has been the experience of a working-class Japanese man whose father died early in his life and who then got a job on the assembly line of an automobile factory?'

When considering national psychologies, we need to remember that these do not need to be taken absolutely literally. When one talks in general terms of the national psychology of Britain or of Japan, one is engaging in a kind of fantasizing process: Britons are reserved, ironic, emotionally repressed, and possessed of 'grace under pressure'; Japanese people are disciplined, obedient, courteous, and unimaginative. Such fantasy needs to be valued as psychically real, even if arguable from a factual point of view. It is not disreputable to speak of fantasy in this way. Fantasies about national psychology exist, and cannot be wished out of existence. Our task is to do something with them. The problem is that this could simply reinforce bigotry and xenophobia. But what if we introduced into our inquiry some kind of cross-referencing so that an Italian's fantasies about a 'typical' Norwegian and the latter's fantasies about the Italian could be kept in parallel at least long enough to permit some reflection on them? We might find lots of projections, or each might say the same thing about the other, or there might be no pattern whatsoever.

At least a kind of balance of power is maintained: no generalization of a psychological kind about the other nation will take place without an equivalent generalization in exchange. It would be fascinating to see what would happen if each fantasy or set of fantasies were elicited and recorded in isolation from the other set. Also, the fantasies need not be only of the other nation. They can be self-reflexive: what does a Brazilian consider Brazilian national psychology to be, and what does a South African consider South African national psychology to be?

Such a project could obviously get quite complicated, especially if the number of national psychologies under consideration were not limited to two – but this is intended as only a sketch of a set of principles upon which inquiry might be based, not a full-scale experimental design.

If we are prepared to acknowledge that differences of a psychological kind exist between nations, we need to be careful about how we organize such speculations. So if 'data' come in suggesting that one national group is X, we need to make sure we do not automatically label a second, historically rivalrous national group as minus X. This complementary tendency ('binomial thinking') has bedevilled many attempts to explore national psychology from a comparative perspective: for example, French thought is abstract and theoretical, British thought is concrete and empirical. If French thought is theoretical, and we have set out to *compare* it with British thought, then whatever stands as the complementary opposite of 'theoretical' becomes the term used to describe British thought. Hence, it might be more accurate to say that, because we have depicted French thought as theoretical, we are forced to depict British thought as empirical.

What this means in practice is that the necessity to compare must be managed very carefully, because it so easily leads to rigid complementary thinking. We can see this problem rather clearly in work that has been done on the psychologies of the two sexes, which has been rendered superficial by the introduction of complementarity in an attempt to compare: men are rational, women irrational; men are good at spatial thinking, women at verbal thinking. There are other ways than complementarity to divide up a field.

If the psychologies of interiority (such as psychoanalysis or analytical psychology) are to address the *external* question of national psychology, then their stock in trade – which is images and everything to do with them – needs to be allowed some sovereignty. The images of political types introduced in Chapter 2 are also useful when considering national psychologies. In such-and-such a context (for example, a war), at such-and-such a time (for example, now as opposed to a hundred years ago), in such-and-such a configuration (for example, in opposition to *this* nation as opposed to *that* nation), a nation operates on the basis of a particular type or group of types. Another nation might operate in a very different way. For example, in the Second World War, it could be said that Britain regarded Germany as a terrorist nation while Germany continued to regard itself as a philosopher nation. Britain saw itself as a restorative healer or warrior nation while Germany saw Britain as exhibitionistic and playing victim to seduce the United States.

The kind of mutual cross-referencing mentioned earlier might also be brought in here, so that any question about the type of one nation would be balanced by a similar question about that of another. This is a game for two or more players.

Finally, can we let nations speak in their own terms about their own psychologies, instead of defining what these might be? Definitions are the very devil here, although they may have a great appeal as a sort of refuge from the massive vagueness that inevitably attends a notion such as national psychology. It might be useful to take a cue from therapists, who have developed the capacity to listen to the narratives of people's experiences in a highly particularized, non-judgemental way. It is in this spirit – anti-definitional, anecdotal, speculative, imaginative and even playful – that the inquiry into national psychologies should be conducted.

I shall conclude by giving a brief description of a small project based on some of these principles. In the mid-1990s, there was a meeting held in Paris of the European Group of Jungian Analysts, attended by representatives from ten countries. Like all analysts, Jungians are incorrigibly disputatious, warring among themselves as well as hostile (or ostentatiously indifferent) to other schools of psychotherapy. Since the theme of the meeting was exploration of our national differences as analysts, it seemed pressing to find out more about the national bases for the ill feeling between us.

Everyone was asked to write several lines about how they imagined or fantasized that a typical analyst from each country (including their own) conducted their practice. Respondents stated their countries of origin on the slips of paper on which they recorded their responses. We therefore ended up with ten sets of responses about each of the ten countries. Then we simply read out all the responses, grouped according to the country being fantasized about, and had a protracted general discussion.

Aside from a noticeable improvement in levels of mutual respect and toleration, plus an increased desire to learn more about the practice of the others, it was noticeable that there was an overall consistency of response when fantasy about the other(s) was the main basis for expression. Hence, for example, what the analysts from the other nine countries said about Italian analysts was very similar. What the Italians said about themselves, however, differed from what all the others said about them. Additionally, like the analysts from every other country, the Italian representatives produced self-descriptions of their own clinical practices that differed greatly from one another's. It appeared that, in this setting and with these players, fantasies about the other could be consistent, whereas fantasies about 'self' tended to vary.

This was, of course, a highly atypical group – everyone had been motivated to attend an international gathering on this theme. Not only were the respondents exceptionally co-operative, at least on the surface, but also two-thirds of them chose to write their responses in English, even though they had been invited to use whichever language they preferred. These conditions would not be replicated in a situation of true international conflict. Therefore, nothing that tran-spired in this microcosm 'proved' anything. But we all felt that something worthwhile had happened to us as a group and as individuals and that, by the end of the experience, nation-based fantasy had been honoured and responsibly le-gitimized. No harm was done.

CHAPTER THIRTEEN

The transformation of politics

Hurrah for revolution and more cannon-shot!
A beggar upon horseback lashes a beggar on foot.
Hurrah for revolution and cannon come again!
The beggars have changed places, but the lash goes on.

W. B. Yeats, 'The Great Day'

ANYONE PROPOSING a change in political arrangements or behaviour should heed the caution in Yeats's
'apolitical' poem. How can we make sure that the
changes we are proposing are not just a matter of the lash
passing from one hand to another?

The vision of political change set forth in this book has its
roots in the principles and practices of psychotherapy. As a
world-view, therapy tends to reject simplistic 'with one
mighty bound he was free' solutions, though, like everyone
else, therapists can be seduced by such solutions. Nevertheless, it can seem like a weakness of psychotherapy that it
tends to go in for too much complexification, piling explanation upon explanation in an over-determined way. The
virtues of the discipline will often look like political vices,
especially in a crisis: caution, delay, reflection as opposed
to action, willingness to see all sides, excessive devotion to

compromise. On one level they *are* vices; but they have the potential to alter fundamentally the way we do politics these days.

A goal of this book is to achieve recognition of the ways in which such psychotherapeutic virtues could be useful to politics and politicians. If people in positions of power, and those in a position to influence public opinion, such as journalists, add perspectives like those outlined in the book to the bank of ideas that they already draw on to formulate and critique policies, therapy will finally have succeeded in changing the world at least a little bit. But marginal political activists, members of single issue social movements, and citizens who have not actually joined anything are as crucial as the powerful to the politics I have in mind. The repositioning of the citizen as a therapist of society and the encouragement to citizens to dwell on their political selfhood and political myth will probably lead, not to acquiescence in present arrangements, but to challenges to them. How people think and feel about politics affects what actually happens.

It was tempting to end the book with a 'manifesto'. But that promise of comprehensiveness and a brand new start is out of keeping with the cautious and modest programme proposed herein: not to claim that psychotherapy has all the answers, but to factor the psychotherapy 'bit' into what exists. We have to start with what we have (a psychotherapy virtue, this) and resist siren calls for a completely different variant of consciousness suddenly to appear, riding to the rescue. This is not to say that consciousness does not change over time; of course it does. The ideas in the book can be understood as part of a much larger gradual shift in thinking about politics in the West that is already closing the gap between the internal life and the political world.

The transformation of politics sought here means that outer world issues will not be looked at as divorced from the personal and subjective lives of the people involved. Transformative politics is also a profound form of self-expression, perhaps on a spiritual level, and requires a new understanding of social action as part of the citizen's individuation (or a lack of commitment to social action as a limitation of individuation). Transformative politics aims at a resacralization of culture, an attempt to generate a sense of meaning and purpose not only in private but also in public life. Power will always be *the* political issue but, in transformative politics, political power is complemented by the concept of political energy. Here, the question is whether and how the citizen or group of citizens is maximally concentrating imagination upon a designated problem – the concern is not only that they might quickly shift the problem or transcend it. The energy lies in and stems from the approach being taken. Political energy of this kind is available to the powerless and may exist in indirect proportion to political power: the less power the more energy, the more power the less energy. 'The race is not to the swift, nor the battle to the strong . . .', in the words of Ecclesiastes. Perhaps that is why powerful leaders seem so uninspiring these days, so diminished in comparison with the degree of power that they have. And if political energy can be tapped into and focused outwards by the powerless, they may find that they do indeed have the means to change some things some of the time.

Transformative politics demands that citizens contemplate themselves as political beings and tell themselves and others evolving versions of their political myths, asking who they are as citizens as well as people. Although it is possible and useful to understand a good deal of political selfhood by exploring the influences of one's past history, there is a dimension (what I called political type) that resists explanation. This is a matter of fate, temperament, innate characteristics – a private, political mystery. Why do people approach politics and see the material world in such amazingly different ways? Why has society become, at times, a battleground over ideas of itself? What is the *telos*, the goal or aim of this chronic human disputatiousness? Does aggression in society indeed mask a secret need for deeper contact, as it sometimes does in personal relationships or marriage? The citizen wanting to embrace transformative politics cannot avoid struggling with these difficult questions. Transformative politics repays the compliment, trusting the political wisdom of citizens who are too modest, diffident, dreamy and, perhaps, downtrodden to claim it.

As far as dispute within society is concerned, could we entertain the idea of a National Institute for Reconciliation (NIR)? Such a body would enable us to apply what psychology (not just psychotherapy) has learned about resolving differences. The courts could make referrals of special cases where emotions have run exceptionally high to the NIR. Crucially, the remit would be not only to attempt to reach an arbitrated settlement but also to try to resolve the dispute in depth, leading to a reconciliation of the warring parties. Failure to reach agreement would not be stigmatized since it would be accepted that too much agreement can spell desiccation and there are also problems with skin-deep agreements reached to keep mediators happy.

Psychotherapy's contribution to transformative politics stems from its overall world-view. But there are a number of psychoanalytic ideas that make a direct contribution. The idea of good-enoughness is a significant addition to the political lexicon. It means avoiding the pitfalls of idealizing or denigrating a leader or citizens idealizing or denigrating themselves. In the latter case, the good-enough citizen is one who can cope with the disappointment of not being as thoughtful about or effective in politics as consciously wished for. Failure to be a perfect citizen would not tip over into excessive civic self-depreciation. It is surprising, in fact, how many political problems respond to the 'good-enough' treatment. What happens when we say that we need a good-enough military, a good-enough economy, a good-enough education system? As soon as the idea of good-enoughness enters in, the expectation of perfection is reduced; the inevitable paralysis that follows on massive disappointment is avoided, and we are therefore more free both to complain and to act. Similarly, at the negative end of the spectrum, the temptation to subside into terminal despair at the disgusting state of things is also reduced; relieved of our feelings of impotence, we become less likely to cede our autonomy and agency to others and more likely to take action ourselves.

Ambivalence is a psychoanalytic concept that characterizes and helps to understand a whole range of developments in contemporary society: relations between the sexes, between siblings, and between children and parents; feelings about wealth creation and inequalities of wealth; attitudes to homosexuality. Ambivalence steers a middle way between love and hate by allowing them to coexist, rather than attempting to deny one or the other and thereby forcing individuals to yet greater extremes. ('Beyond every fanaticism lurks a secret doubt,' said Jung.) Accepting the inevitability of ambivalence enables us to welcome the passions into political discourse without fear that they will take it over.

Finally, in this homage to psychotherapy we come to the

unconscious, or to the psyche itself: source of the problems we face, and source of fresh and constructive ways to address them. The psyche is both radical and conservative, benevolent and malevolent, constructive and destructive. Nowhere are the contradictions of human experience better demonstrated than in the operations of the psyche itself. The psyche may be constituted and irradiated by ambivalence, but it is still a good-enough psyche.

Yet these strands of thinking, taken from psychotherapy, must not be allowed to stand in for a full-scale politics – that is also why I have not called this concluding chapter a manifesto. Full-scale politics needs to regard perspectives from psychotherapy as highly desirable, if not yet absolutely essential add-ons. Also needed are progressive and imaginative perspectives from economics, social science, the arts and humanities and religion. Keeping the limitations of the psychotherapy approach in mind allows us to acknowledge its potential for opening up a political two-way street – the term I coined to allow the secret psychological life of politics to be explored in parallel with a search for the secret politics of psychological life. At times, any psychotherapist commenting on politics is going to slip into psychological triumphalism – and should expect to be slapped down for it. But this slippage is no worse than accounts of the political that have nothing to do with people's subjective experiences, hence slapping down their experiences of the world. Under transformative politics, many new dimensions of the relationships between leaders and led will emerge, including a dismantling of the structures that differentiate them (sibling politics). Leaders who are good-enough will be profoundly implicated in failure, they will study why they did not or could not do what they had wanted to do and communicate the results of their study to the citizenry. Everyone will start to speak a language of failure and the management of disappointment. When citizens conceive of themselves as citizens-as-therapists, the burdens of responsibility will be shared.

Let us fantasize about implementing a National Failure Enquiry which would continuously monitor why initiatives have not worked out as planned. Members of the main political parties would sit on the NFE, whose proceedings would be widely circulated. Its function would not be to apportion blame but to try to understand as fully as possible what happened, come to terms with it and learn lessons for the future. This new approach to failure would mean that citizens will lose the 'out' of blaming leaders or the system, but get a greater opportunity to mould the world in which they and their friends, workmates and children live. As therapists of the world, citizens have a basis from which to debate the state's usual claim to be the sum of what happens within it – the containing mother model of the state. Thinking afresh about the relations of the One and the Many showed us that the state is, at times, a One happening within the Many. Its desire to unify and regulate diversity, imposing order by law (the juridical father model of the state) can also be seen through and made into a topic for debate.

What about a National Diversity Commission to enable members of the different minority communities to share their experiences with each other and with members of the so-called majority community? The NDC would also be a place where the differing interests of women and men (and children) would be paid attention. Special topics for its early consideration would be male powerlessness and homophobia (for reasons that have been explained in the book). The Commission would establish fora where members of single issue social movements and similar groups could dialogue with each other. A fourth aspect of the NDC's work would be to set up an inquiry into national identity and psychology – in the UK, this would be for the country as a whole as well as for England, Scotland, Wales and Northern Ireland. Lastly, the NDC would do its best to benefit people living in lone-parent families or other, statistically less 'normal' kinds of family organizations. It would accomplish this by collecting testimony, establishing research projects and advocating new attitudes and policies. The NDC would be assisted by psychotherapists including therapists who come from ethnic and other minority backgrounds.

Transformative politics, associated as it is with psychology, breeds a psychological economics. At the heart of economics is a debate about human nature, one that is decisive when it comes to the formation of economic policy. Psychotherapists know that human beings are creative, collaborative, caring, co-operative – and the shadowy opposite of those things: greedy, opportunistic, ruthless, destructive. They enjoy and suffer this bothness. Hence the psychology that informs the debate over human nature (central to the economy) has to be a psychology of bothness. That is why the economic proposals discussed in the book were bound to be contradictory.

Could we imagine a National Emotional Audit to assess other ways of marking progress in the economic and social realms besides statistical and financial reckonings? The emotional aspects of economic life are difficult to measure but, up to now, this has not been tried. The audit would encompass questions of environmental desirability, sustainability and aesthetics because these are the main psychological axes of economics. It would explore the limits on wealth that the community seeks to establish and inquire into obvious disparities and anomalies in income – for example, why carers continue to be so badly paid. It would research the impact on psychological health of living in an economically polarized society – for the rich, the poor and those with middle incomes. The audit's task would include the monitoring of vocational retraining programmes conducted by the government or other bodies to make sure that these are not too instrumental but adopt a wider and more humane attitude to 'education'. The membership of the NEA would include psychotherapists, health professionals and educators, people from religious backgrounds and artists – as well as economists and social scientists with a range of points of view.

A new approach to spirituality is required for transformative politics to reach its potential. This includes understanding spirituality as an expression of a profoundly democratic commitment to equality – equality in the eyes of God being translated into equality in society. Craft spirituality understands that there is no need to relegate the world of work and the processes of manufacture to a non-spiritual or anti-spiritual box. Human beings have a genius for being artificial; it is their defining characteristic and not a moral failing. Spirituality has its profane dimension as well, and transformative politics engenders an approach to spirituality that can descry it in what seem like psychopathology and immaturity. But the syndromes and symptoms of psychotherapy and psychiatry do not cause their possessors to be cast out of the spiritual lifeboat. The stone that the builder rejected . . .

Let us play with the idea of an Emotional and Spiritual Justice Commission that would monitor the effects on psychological and spiritual health of all policy proposals. We have seen how policy decisions affect people's self-esteem and self-respect and regulate how easy or difficult it is to establish links with other people. Arrangements could be made to allow anyone who wanted to tell the story of how their private space has been affected by public policy to communicate with the commission. Adherents of the various formal religions would sit on the ESJC alongside health professionals, psychotherapists and members of the general public.

Many people from disciplines other than politics want to contribute to society as citizens alongside the less direct contribution they make as specialists. Innumerable artists, writers, scientists, doctors, business people, craft workers and religious people come to mind. We saw that Freud and Jung were no different. People feel impelled from within by a sense of responsibility or are driven by conscience or have had personal experiences that thrust them towards the political. All of us are moved by a political drive that we can no more opt out of or ignore than we can other drives such as sex and aggression. In order to flourish in our day jobs and family lives we have to make commitments that go beyond the job and the needs of intimates – commitments to work towards fulfilling the needs and desires of strangers.

Each contributor or potential contributor to politics has to develop a sense of the space in which the politics they believe in can take place. Usually this will be a safe and contained place, but not a hermetically sealed one, lest innovation and movement be stifled. In psychoanalytic language, such a space is called a facilitating environment and, in early life, the facilitating environment is provided by humans – parents or other early caretakers. But facilitating environments, even for babies, are characterized by more than the human presences they contain. They have their particular atmosphere and form, hidden and open principles, social systems, and visual, acoustic and sensory imagery. All of these are essential to an 'environment'. The facilitating environment for transformative politics will also be formed of human and non-human components, some quite rational and susceptible to measurement and some definitely not. This environment's primary values will be respect for others ambivalently coupled with self-respect and self-assertion, together with compassion in the face of failure.

Attempts are constantly made to improve the facilitating environment for politics, usually by redistributing wealth or changing legislative and constitutional structures. Such projects are necessary and valuable and will generate their own psychological changes. The consequences of effective and fair minimum wage legislation or devolving power to the regions of a country will have effects that show up on any National Emotional Audit. But a materialist approach deriving exclusively from economics, or one that depends solely on altering the structures of the state, will not refresh those parts of the individual citizen or the people that a psychological perspective can reach. Our disappointment at liberal democracy's failure to deliver the goods and our growing realization that there are limits to what can be achieved by economic redistribution or altering the constitution strengthen this book's argument: something is missing in contemporary politics that has led to a calamitous denial of the secret life at its core. We can change the clothes, shift the pieces around, but the spectre that haunts materialist and constitutional moves in the political world is that they only ruffle the surface and do not (because, alone, they cannot) bring about the transformations for which the political soul yearns.

I recognize fully that the depth perspectives I am advocating here may never be applied to our political culture.

Everything I have said may fail to make one iota of difference to the condition of the world. So I will end with a few words by Samuel Beckett, who lived and worked as closely as anyone with the need to go on in the face of not being able to go on: 'No matter. Try again. Fail again. Fail better.'

Notes

1 THE SECRET LIFE OF POLITICS

1 Sigmund Freud, 'The claims of psycho-analysis to
   scientific interest', in Vol. 13, *Standard Edition of the
   Complete Psychological Works of Sigmund Freud*
   (London: Hogarth Press, 1953–73), pp. 185–6.
2 C. G. Jung, Preface to *Essays on Contemporary Events*, in
   Vol. 10, *Collected Works of C. G. Jung*, (London:
   Routledge and Kegan Paul; Princeton, NJ; Princeton
   University Press, 1952) p. 187.
3 See Ian Craib, *Psychoanalysis and Social Theory: The
   Limits of Sociology* (London and New York: Harvester
   Wheatsheaf, 1989). Peter Homans, *The Ability to Mourn:
   Disillusionment and the Social Origins of Psychoanalysis*
   (Chicago: University of Chicago Press, 1989).
4 Neil Altman, *The Analyst in the Inner City: Race, Class,
   and Culture through a Psychoanalytic Lens* (Hillsdale, NJ:
   Analytic Press, 1995). Philip Cushman, *Constructing the
   Self, Constructing America: A Cultural History of
   Psychotherapy* (Reading, MA.: Addison-Wesley, 1995).
5 See Louise Eichenbaum and Susie Orbach, *Outside In . . .
   Inside Out: Women's Psychology: A Feminist Psychoanalytic*

Approach (Harmondsworth: Penguin, 1982). Susie Orbach, 'Beyond the grand emotions: the challenge of disappointment' (unpublished, 1998). Claudette Kulkarni, *Lesbians and Lesbianisms: A Post-Jungian Perspective* (London and New York: Routledge, 1997).

6 James Hillman and Michael Ventura, *We've Had a Hundred Years of Psychotherapy and the World is Getting Worse* (San Francisco: Harper, 1992).

7 Nikolas Rose, *Governing the Soul: The Shaping of the Private Self* (London: Routledge, 1990).

8 See the extensive review in Richard Tillett, 'Psychotherapy assessment and treatment selection', *British Journal of Psychiatry*, Vol. 168, 1996, pp. 10–15.

9 Theodore Roszak, *The Voice of the Earth: An Exploration of Ecopsychology* (London: Bantam, 1993).

2 THE POLITICS OF TRANSFORMATION

1 Oscar Wilde, 'The soul of man under socialism', in *Complete Works of Oscar Wilde* (London: Book Club Associates, 1978), p. 1010.

4 THE SECRET POLITICS OF THE INTERNAL FAMILY

1 C. G. Jung, *Symbols of Transformation*, in Vol. 10, *Collected Works of C. G. Jung*, pp. 348–9. Written in 1911–12.

2 Roszika Parker, *Torn in Two: The Experience of Maternal Ambivalence* (London: Virago, 1995).

3 For example, Elizabeth Keller, *A Feeling for the Organism: The Life and Work of Barbara McLintock* (New York: Freeman, 1983). Hilary Rose, *Love, Power and Knowledge: Towards a Feminist Transformation of the Sciences* (Cambridge: Polity Press, 1994).

4 Sara Ruddick, *Maternal Thinking: Towards the Politics of Peace* (Boston, MA: Beacon Press, 1989). It is a great pity that this inspiring book has not entered the mainstream of political thinking.

5 THE SECRET PSYCHOLOGY OF POLITICAL FORMS

1 See Jacques Lacan, 'Seminar of 21 January 1975', in Juliet Mitchell and Jacqueline Rose (eds), *Feminine Sexuality: Jacques Lacan and the Ecole Freudienne* (London: Macmillan, 1982), pp. 162–71: 'Good form and meaning are akin'.

2 Richard Dawkins, *The Extended Phenotype* (Oxford: Oxford University Press, 1982).

3 Stuart Hall, 'Deviance, politics and the media', in H. Abelove, M. Barale and D. Halperin (eds), *The Lesbian and Gay Studies Reader* (London and New York: Routledge, 1993), p. 85.

4 C. G. Jung, *The Psychology of the Transference*, in Vol. 16, *Collected Works of C. G. Jung*, p. 224. Written in 1946.

5 Jung, *Psychology of the Transference*, p. 233.

6 Andrew Samuels, *The Political Psyche* (London and New York: Routledge, 1993), pp. 125–75.

7 Eve Kosofsky Sedgwick, *Between Men: English Literature and Male Homosocial Desire* (New York: Columbia

University Press, 1985).

8 Lynne Segal, *Slow Motion: Changing Masculinities,
   Changing Men* (London: Virago, 1990).

6 THE GOOD-ENOUGH LEADER

1 C. G. Jung, Preface to *Essays on Contemporary Events*, in
   Vol. 10, *Collected Works of C. G. Jung*, p. 187. Written in
   1946. Sigmund Freud, 'The claims of psycho-analysis to
   scientific interest', in Vol. 13, *Standard Edition of the
   Complete Psychological Works of Sigmund Freud* (London:
   Hogarth Press, 1953–73), pp. 185–6.

2 Shanto Iyengar and William J. McGuire (eds),
   Explorations in Political Psychology (Durham, NC and
   London: Duke University Press, 1993).

3 James Hillman, *The Myth of Analysis* (New York: Harper,
   1968).

4 Ulrich Beck, *Risk Society: Towards a New Modernity*
   (London: Sage, 1992).

5 Andrew Samuels, *The Plural Psyche: Personality, Morality
   and the Father* (London and New York: Routledge, 1989);
   The Political Psyche (London and New York: Routledge,
   1993).

6 Homi Bhaba (ed.), *Nation and Narration* (London and
   New York: Routledge, 1992). Michael Vannoy Adams, *The
   Multicultural Imagination: 'Race', Color and the
   Unconscious* (London and New York: Routledge, 1996).

7 Jean Laplanche, *Life and Death in Analysis* (Baltimore,
   MD: Johns Hopkins University Press, 1976).

7 THE GOOD-ENOUGH FATHER OF WHATEVER SEX

1   Walter Seccombe, *Weathering the Storm: The History of Working Class Families* (London: Verso, 1993). Helen Wilkinson, 'Celebrate the new family', *New Statesman*, 9 August 1999.

2   Charles Murray, 'Underclass', in Digby Anderson (ed.), *Family Portraits* (London: Social Affairs Unit, 1990). Wilkinson, 'Celebrate the new family'.

3   Joan Rivière, 'Womanliness as masquerade', *Int. J. Psycho-Anal.*, Vol. 10, 1929, pp. 35–44.

4   Michel Foucault, *The History of Sexuality* (London: Allen Lane, 1979–88). Jeffrey Weeks, *Sexuality and its Discontents* (London and New York: Routledge, 1985).

5   Joan Raphael-Leff, *Psychological Processes of Childbearing* (London and New York: Chapman and Hall, 1991), pp. 372, 533.

6   Judith Butler, *Gender Trouble: Feminism and the Subversion of Identity* (London and New York: Routledge, 1990).

7   Jonathan Dollimore, *Sexual Dissidence: Augustine to Wilde* (Oxford: Oxford University Press, 1991).

8   Donald Winnicott, 'Mind and its relation to the psyche-soma', in *Through Paediatrics to Psychoanalysis* (London: Hogarth Press, 1958). Written in 1949. Winnicott, 'The effect of psychotic parents on the emotional development of the child', in *The Family and Individual Development* (London: Tavistock, 1968).

9   See also the 'Bowlby complex' of the 1960s where some mothers were said not to leave their children alone because of what the psychoanalyst John Bowlby had said

about separation.

10 Donald Winnicott, 'What about father?', in *Getting to Know Your Baby* (London: Heinemann, 1944).

11 Margaret Mahler, 'A study of the separation-individuation process', *Psychol. Stud. Child*, 1971, pp. 401–27.

12 Judith Jordan *et al. Women's Growth in Connection: Writings from the Stone Center* (New York and London: Guilford, 1991).

13 Jacques Lacan, *Ecrits* (trans. Alan Sheridan) (London: Tavistock, 1977).

14 John Forrester, *The Seductions of Psychoanalysis: Freud, Lacan, and Derrida* (Cambridge: Cambridge University Press, 1990), pp. 110–11.

15 Elizabeth Badinger, *The Myth of Motherhood: An Historical View of the Maternal Instinct* (London: Souvenir Press, 1981).

8 POLITICS, SPIRITUALITY, PSYCHOTHERAPY

1 Timothy Williamson, *Vagueness* (London and New York: Routledge, 1994).

2 Exodus 37: 1–5.

3 Richard Zaehner, *Mysticism Sacred and Profane* (Oxford: Oxford University Press, 1957).

4 Bani Shorter, *Susceptible to the Sacred* (London and New York, Routledge, 1995).

5 John Rawls, *A Theory of Justice* (Cambridge, MA.: Belknap Press, 1971).

9 THE ECONOMIC PSYCHE

1 Joan Rivière, 'Womanliness as masquerade', *Int. J. Psycho-Anal.*, Vol. 10, 1929, pp. 35–44.
2 Andrew Samuels, *The Political Psyche* (London and New York, Routledge, 1993), pp. 88–94.
3 These are some of the questions explored at workshops on 'the economic psyche':
    1 What are the three most pressing economic problems facing the US (or UK)?
    2 What are your solutions?
    3 What are the three most pressing economic problems facing the world?
    4 What are your solutions?
    5 Do you find economics mystifying?
    6 What aspects of economics would you like to know more about?
    7 In what format would you like to learn more – e.g. distance learning, seminars, etc.?
    8 How much more taxation would you be prepared to pay if you approved of what the money would do?
    9 What things would you prefer not to pay taxes for?
    10 What are your feelings and attitudes towards the very wealthy?
    11 Do you feel that economic issues have got out of the control of our government?
    12 What can be done about unemployment?
    13 Do you agree that we should not consume more resources than we can replace?
    14 If this means giving something up, what could you give up?
    15 What are your memories of money issues in your

childhood?

16 How did your family handle money?

17 Was money talked about at home?

18 Have you 'done better' than your parent(s)?

19 How do you feel about the answer to the last question?

20 How do you handle money issues in your personal relationships now?

21 Have you ever had fantasies about having lots of money?

22 What are they?

23 Do you feel guilty about economic inequalities in the world – e.g. between First and Third World countries?

24 Do you think we in the West should draw back economically speaking?

25 Would you say that money and economic matters have injured the values you would like to stick to?

4 Andrew Samuels, *Political Psyche*, pp. 201–6.

5 Russell Lockhart, 'Coins and psychological change', in John Beebe (ed.), *Money, Food, Drink and Fashion and Analytical Training: Depth Dimensions of Physical Existence* (Fellbach-Oeffingen: Bonz Verlag, 1983), pp. 22–7.

10 THE POLITICAL CLINIC

1 Eric Raynor, *The Independent Mind in British Psychoanalysis* (London: Free Association Books, 1991). Edward Slatker (ed.), *Countertransference: A Comprehensive View of those Reactions of the Therapist to the Patient that may Help or Hinder the Treatment* (Northdale, NJ: Jason Aronson, 1987).

2 Andrew Samuels, *The Plural Psyche: Personality, Morality and the Father* (London and New York: Routledge, 1989), pp. 161–97.

3 Christopher Bollas, *The Shadow of the Object: Psychoanalysis of the Unthought Known* (London: Free Association Books, 1987), p. 208.

4 Richard Kuhns, *Psychoanalytic Theory of Art* (New York: Columbia University Press, 1983). Ellen Spitz, *Art and Psyche* (New Haven, CT: Yale University Press, 1985).

5 Karl Figlio, 'Oral history and the unconscious', *History Workshop*, Vol. 26, 1988, pp. 1–28.

6 Joan Chodorow, *Dance Therapy and Depth Psychology: The Moving Imagination* (London and New York: Routledge, 1991). Kristina Stanton, 'Dance movement therapy: an introduction', *British J. Occupational Therapy*, Vol. 54, No. 3, 1991, pp. 42–59. Wendy Wyman, 'The body as a manifestation of unconscious experience' (unpublished, 1991). and especially Ilene Serlin, 'Kinaesthetic imagining: a phenomenological study' (unpublished, 1989).

7 Russell Jacoby, *The Repression of Psychoanalysis: Otto Fenichel and the Political Freudians* (New York: Basic Books, 1983), p. 32.

11 PSYCHOTHERAPY, THE CITIZEN AND THE STATE

1 See Renos Papadopoulos, 'Jung and the concept of the Other', in Renos Papadoupolos and Graham Saayman (eds), *Jung in Modern Perspective: The Legacy of the Master* (Bridport, Dorset: Prism, 1991).

2 Donald Winnicott, *Playing and Reality* (New York: Penguin, 1971), p. 117.

12 EXPLORING NATIONAL PSYCHOLOGIES

1 Quoted in Peregrine Worsthorne, 'Why I'm no longer a nationalist', *New Statesman*, 16 August 1999.

Bibliography

Adams, Michael Vannoy, *The Multicultural Imagination: 'Race', Color and the Unconscious*. London and New York: Routledge, 1996.

Altman, Neil, *The Analyst in the Inner City: Race, Class, and Culture through a Psychoanalytic Lens*. Hillsdale, NJ: Analytic Press, 1995.

Anderson, Digby (ed.), *Family Portraits*. London: Social Affairs Unit, 1990.

Badinger, Elizabeth, *The Myth of Motherhood: An Historical View of the Maternal Instinct*. London: Souvenir Press, 1981.

Beck, Ulrich, *Risk Society: Towards a New Modernity*. London: Sage, 1992.

Beebe, John (ed.), *Money, Food, Drink and Fashion and Analytical Training: Depth Dimensions of Physical Existence*. Fellbach-Oeffingen: Bonz Verlag, 1983.

Bhaba, Homi (ed.), *Nation and Narration*. London and New York: Routledge, 1992.

Bollas, Christopher, *The Shadow of the Object: Psychoanalysis of the Unthought Known*. London: Free Association Books, 1987.

Brown, Dennis and Zinkin, Louis, *The Psyche and the*

World: Developments in Group-Analytic Theory. London and New York: Routledge, 1994.

Butler, Judith, *Gender Trouble: Feminism and the Subversion of Identity*. London and New York: Routledge, 1990.

Chodorow, Joan, *Dance Therapy and Depth Psychology: The Moving Imagination*. London and New York: Routledge, 1991.

Craib, Ian, *Psychoanalysis and Social Theory: The Limits of Sociology*. London and New York: Harvester Wheatsheaf, 1989.

Cushman, Philip, *Constructing the Self, Constructing America: A Cultural History of Psychotherapy*. Reading, MA: Addison-Wesley, 1995.

Dawkins, Richard, *The Extended Phenotype*. Oxford: Oxford University Press, 1982.

Dollimore, Jonathan, *Sexual Dissidence: Augustine to Wilde*. Oxford: Oxford University Press, 1991.

du Bois, Page, *Sowing the Body: Psychoanalysis and Ancient Representations of Women*. Chicago: University of Chicago Press, 1988.

Eichenbaum, Louise and Orbach, Susie, *Outside In . . . Inside Out: Women's Psychology: A Feminist Psychoanalytic Approach*. Harmondsworth: Penguin, 1982.

Figlio, Karl, 'Oral history and the unconscious', *History Workshop*, Vol. 26, 1988, pp. 1–28.

Forrester, John, *The Seductions of Psychoanalysis: Freud, Lacan, and Derrida*. Cambridge: Cambridge University Press, 1990.

Foucault, Michel, *The History of Sexuality*. London: Allen Lane, 1979–88.

Freud, Sigmund, 'The claims of psycho-analysis to scientific interest', in Vol. 13, *Standard Edition of the Complete Psychological Works of Sigmund Freud*. London: Hogarth Press, 1953–73.

Hall, Stuart, 'Deviance, politics and the media', in H. Abelove, M. Barale and D. Halperin (eds), *The Lesbian and Gay Studies Reader*. London and New York: Routledge, 1993.

Hillman, James, *The Myth of Analysis*. New York: Harper, 1968.

Hillman, James and Ventura, Michael, *We've Had a Hundred Years of Psychotherapy and the World is Getting Worse*. San Francisco: Harper, 1992.

Homans, Peter, *The Ability to Mourn: Disillusionment and the Social Origins of Psychoanalysis*. Chicago: University of Chicago Press, 1989.

Iyengar, Shanto and McGuire, William J. (eds), *Explorations in Political Psychology*. Durham, NC and London: Duke University Press, 1993.

Jacoby, Russell, *The Repression of Psychoanalysis: Otto Fenichel and the Political Freudians*. New York: Basic Books, 1983.

Jordan, Judith *et al.*, *Women's Growth in Connection: Writings from the Stone Center*. New York and London: Guilford, 1991.

Jung, C. G.: Except where indicated, references are by volume and page number to the *Collected Works* (*CW*) of C. G. Jung, 20 Vols. (eds Herbert Read, Michael Fordham and Gerhard Adler; trans. R. F. C. Hull). London and Princeton, NJ: Routledge and Kegan Paul and Princeton University Press, 1953–77.

Jung, C. G., *Symbols of Transformation*, in Vol. 10, *CW*.

Jung, C. G., Preface to *Essays on Contemporary Events*, in Vol. 10, *CW*.

Jung, C. G., *The Psychology of the Transference*, in Vol. 16, *CW*.

Keller, Elizabeth, *A Feeling for the Organism: The Life and Work of Barbara McLintock*. New York: Freeman, 1983.

Kuhns, Richard, *Psychoanalytic Theory of Art*. New York: Columbia University Press, 1983.

Kulkarni, Claudette, *Lesbians and Lesbianisms: A Post-Jungian Perspective*. London and New York: Routledge, 1997.

Lacan, Jacques, 'Seminar of 21 January 1975', in Juliet Mitchell and Jacqueline Rose (eds), *Feminine Sexuality: Jacques Lacan and the Ecole Freudienne*. London: Macmillan, 1982. Written in 1975.

Lacan, Jacques, *Ecrits* (trans. Alan Sheridan). London: Tavistock, 1977.

Laplanche, Jean, *Life and Death in Analysis*. Baltimore, MD: Johns Hopkins University Press, 1976.

Levine, Howard, Jacobs, D. and Rubin, L. (eds), *Psychoanalysis and the Nuclear Threat: Clinical and Theoretical Studies*. Hillsdale, NJ: Jason Aronson, 1988.

Lewes, Kenneth, *The Psychoanalytic Theory of Male Homosexuality*. New York: Penguin, 1988.

Lockhart, Russell, 'Coins and psychological change', in John Beebe (ed.), *Money, Food, Drink and Fashion and Analytical Training: Depth Dimensions of Physical Existence*. Fellbach-Oeffingen: Bonz Verlag, 1983.

Mahler, Margaret, 'A study of the separation-individuation process', *Psychol. Stud. Child*, 1971, pp. 401–27.

Mitchell, Juliet and Rose, Jacqueline (eds), *Feminine Sexuality: Jacques Lacan and the Ecole Freudienne*. London: Macmillan, 1982.

Murray, Charles, 'Underclass', in Digby Anderson (ed.), *Family Portraits*. London: Social Affairs Unit, 1990.

Orbach, Susie, 'Beyond the grand emotions: the challenge of disappointment', unpublished, 1998.

Papadopoulos, Renos, 'Jung and the concept of the Other', in Renos Papadopoulos and Graham Saayman (eds), *Jung in Modern Perspective: The Master and his Legacy*. Bridport, Dorset: Prism, 1991.

Parker, Roszika, *Torn in Two: The Experience of Maternal Ambivalence*. London: Virago, 1995.

Raphael-Leff, Joan, *Psychological Processes of Childbearing*. London and New York: Chapman and Hall, 1991.

Rawls, John, *A Theory of Justice*. Cambridge, MA.: Belknap Press, 1971.

Raynor, Eric, *The Independent Mind in British Psychoanalysis*. London: Free Association Books, 1991.

Rivière, Joan, 'Womanliness as masquerade', *Int. J. Psycho-Anal.*, Vol. 10, 1929, pp. 35–44.

Rodman, F. Robert (ed.), *The Spontaneous Gesture: Selected Letters of D. W. Winnicott*. Cambridge, MA: Harvard University Press, 1987.

Rose, Hilary, *Love, Power and Knowledge: Towards a Feminist Transformation of the Sciences*. Cambridge: Polity Press, 1994.

Rose, Nikolas, *Governing the Soul: The Shaping of the Private Self*. London: Routledge, 1990.

Roszak, Theodore, *The Voice of the Earth: An Exploration of Ecopsychology*. London: Bantam, 1993.

Ruddick, Sara, *Maternal Thinking: Towards the Politics of Peace*. Boston, MA: Beacon Press, 1989.

Samuels, Andrew, *Jung and the Post-Jungians*. London: Routledge and Kegan Paul, 1985.

Samuels, Andrew, *The Plural Psyche: Personality, Morality and the Father*. London and New York: Routledge, 1989.

Samuels, Andrew, *The Political Psyche*. London and New York: Routledge, 1993.

Samuels, Andrew, 'Replies to an international questionnaire on political material brought into the clinical setting by clients of psychotherapists and analysts', *Int. Rev. Sociology*, Vol. 3, 1994, pp. 7–60.

Seccombe, Walter, *Weathering the Storm: The History of Working Class Families*. London: Verso, 1993.

Sedgwick, Eve Kosofsky, *Between Men: English Literature and Male Homosocial Desire*. New York: Columbia University Press, 1985.

Segal, Lynne, *Slow Motion: Changing Masculinities, Changing Men*. London: Virago, 1990.

Serlin, Ilene, 'Kinaesthetic imagining: a phenomenological study'. Unpublished, 1989.

Shorter, Bani, *Susceptible to the Sacred*. London and New York: Routledge, 1995.

Slatker, Edward (ed.), *Countertransference: A Comprehensive View of those Reactions of the Therapist to the Patient that may Help or Hinder the Treatment*. Northdale, NJ: Jason Aronson, 1987.

Spitz, Ellen, *Art and Psyche*. New Haven, CT: Yale University Press, 1985.

Stanton, Kristina, 'Dance movement therapy: an introduction', *British J. Occupational Therapy* , Vol. 54, No. 3, 1991, pp. 42–59.

Stern, Daniel, *The Interpersonal World of the Infant: A View from Psychoanalysis and Developmental Psychology*. New York: Basic Books, 1985.

Tillett, Richard, 'Psychotherapy assessment and treatment selection'. *British Journal of Psychiatry*, Vol. 168, 1996, pp. 10–15.

Weeks, Jeffrey, *Sexuality and its Discontents*. London and New York: Routledge, 1985.

Wilde, Oscar, 'The soul of man under socialism', in *Complete Works of Oscar Wilde*. London: Book Club Associates, 1978.

Wilkinson, Helen, 'Celebrate the new family', *New Statesman*, 9 August 1999.

Williamson, Timothy, *Vagueness*. London and New York: Routledge, 1994.

Winnicott, Donald, *Getting to Know Your Baby*. London: Heinemann, 1944.

Winnicott, Donald, 'What about father?', in *Getting to Know Your Baby*. London: Heinemann, 1944.

Winnicott, Donald, *Through Paediatrics to Psychoanalysis*. London: Hogarth Press, 1958.

Winnicott, Donald, 'Mind and its relation to the psyche-soma', in *Through Paediatrics to Psychoanalysis*. London: Hogarth Press, 1958. Written in 1949.

Winnicott, Donald, *The Family and Individual Development*. London: Tavistock, 1968.

Winnicott, Donald, 'The effect of psychotic parents on the emotional development of the child', in *The Family and Individual Development*. London: Tavistock, 1968.

Winnicott, Donald, *Playing and Reality*. New York: Penguin, 1971.

Winnicott, Donald, in F. Robert Rodman (ed.), *The Spontaneous Gesture: Selected Letters of D. W. Winnicott*. Cambridge, MA: Harvard University Press, 1987, p. 35.

Worsthorne, Peregrine, 'Why I'm no longer a nationalist', *New Statesman*, 16 August 1999.

Wyman, Wendy, 'The body as a manifestation of unconscious experience'. Unpublished, 1991.

Zaehner, Richard, *Mysticism Sacred and Profane*. Oxford: Oxford University Press, 1957.

Index

A

aesthetics 56
aggression
    paternal 58–9, 68, 112–15
    in society 176, 198
alcohol abuse 128
*Alternative Economic
    Indicators* 145
Altman, Neil 207
ambivalence 38, 61, 199
Anasi 92
anti-nuclear protestors 96
Apollo, and Hermes 73, 92
Ark of the Covenant 126–7
audits
    emotional 152, 202–3
    social 150–51

B

Badinger, Elizabeth 212
Beck, Ulrich 83, 210
Bhaba, Homi 210

Bollas, Christopher 215
Bowlby, John 211
brother–brother political
    forms 71–4
brotherhoods 72–3
brotherliness 72, 73
brother–sister relationship
    59–63, 97
Butler, Judith 211

C

Chodorow, Joan 215
Churchill, Winston 4
citizens
    and the state 175–80
    as therapists 163, 166–7,
      168
class, social 28–9
clinics, political 162–5
Clinton, Bill 4
community 131
competition, in society 177–8

227

M

Machiavelli, N. 77, 80, 92
Mahler, Margaret 118, 212
'male deal, the' 43–4
manufactured world, and
  spirituality 126–7
market economy 141–2
Maslow, Abraham 6
McGuire, William 210
media, the 4
men
  employment and
    flexibility 139–40
  the 'male deal' 43–4
  and political forms 64–74
  and politics 36–8
  see also fathers; gender
Middlemarch (George Eliot)
  21
Midrash 48
modified marketeers 145–6
money
  etymology 158
  see also wealth
mothers 108
  in the fathering role 106,
    108–12
  lone 102, 104–12, 114
  mother–father
    relationship 47–53
  son–mother relationship
    53–7

Mothers of the Plaza de
  Mayo 95
movements
  fundamentalist religious
    18–19
  single-issue
    transformative groups
    25–6
  social 17–18
Murray, Charles 211
Mysticism, Sacred and
  Profane (R. Zaehner) 127

N

National Diversity
  Commission 201–2
National Emotional Audit
  202–3
National Failure Enquiry 201
National Institute for
  Reconciliation 198
national psychologies 186–94
nature, human, and politics
  33–4, 202
networks, social and cultural
  17–18
new deal 35
New Left (1960s) 25

O

Opposition, political 178
Orbach, Susie 7, 130–31, 207

raising children alone 102,
109–10, 111–12, 114
and a sibling mode of
politics 62–3
see also gender; mothers

Wyman, Wendy 215

Z

Zaehner, Richard 212